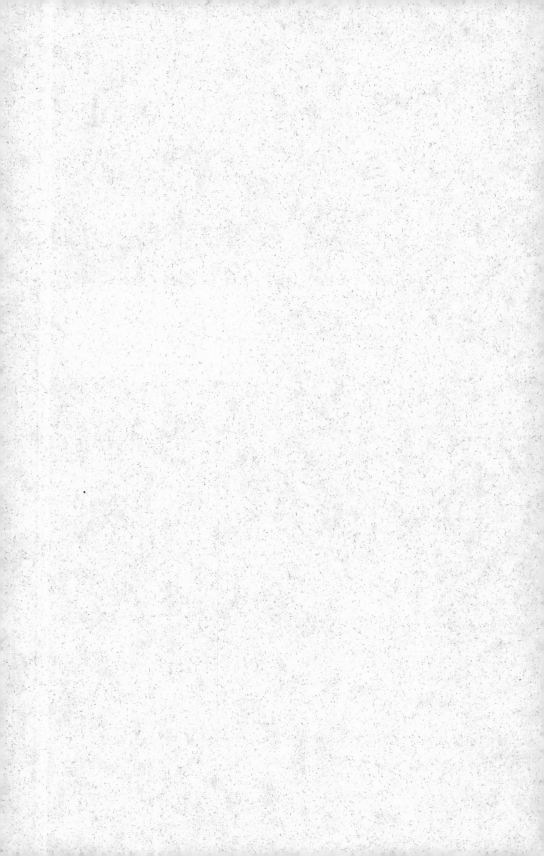

Sleeping Like A Baby

Sleeping Like A Baby

INVESTING IN VOLATILE MARKETS

John C. Hudelson

Published by
Lighthouse Publishing Group, Inc.
Seattle, Washington

Thanks to colleagues past and present for allowing me to learn from and with them. Also my appreciation to my father, Paul, and the others who spent their time reading drafts and providing insight. Most of all, thanks to my clients, without you I would never have experienced this thing we call the market.

Library of Congress Cataloging-in-Publication Data

Hudelson, John C:
Sleeping Like A Baby: Investing in Volatile Markets/John C. Hudelson
p. cm.
1. Investments--Handbooks, manuals, etc.
I. Title.
HG4527.H83 1998 332.6--dc21 98-10062
ISBN (cloth) 0-910019-62-2

Book Design by Judy Burkhalter
Dust Jacket by Angela Wilson

Published by Lighthouse Publishing Group, Inc.
14675 Interurban Avenue South
Seattle, WA 98168-4664
1-800-706-8657

Printed in the United States of America
First Edition
10 9 8 7 6 5 4 3 2 1

When an economist referred to him as an audacious gambler, Mulligan said, "The reason why you'll never get rich is because you think that what I do is gambling."

— Ayn Rand

Atlas Shrugged

To Kari

Contents

Preface

I had been employed on Wall Street for a total of three days when I began to discover that it is a place like no other, because it is not a place—it is a culture, albeit an uncivilized and occasionally unenlightened one. On that morning, my new firm had just completed an offering that had been very lucrative, and everyone was in a great mood. The president of the company came down to the trading floor and loudly announced, "I'm not sure where you guys are on the evolutionary ladder, but you're definitely not human ... you're animals! Keep it up!"

The whole room, full of apparent sub-humans, erupted with appreciative screaming. I began wondering if I had made the right choice of careers as I watched people in thousand dollar suits throw pencils, blow bubble gum, and make innuendos that would make a convict blush.

I quickly learned that Wall Street is inhabited by predators... and then everyone else, who spend most of their time trying to avoid the fate of prey. As Finley Peter Dunne said, "High finance isn't burglary or obtaining money by false pretenses, but rather a judicious selection from the best features of those fine arts."

Well, it's really not that bad. Though there is the occasional case of fraud, manipulation, or other dishonesty, predators on Wall Street account for only a small portion of the losses that investors experience. Those who try to take advantage of investors or manipulate the market deserve severe punishment.

As an explanation for a portfolio's failure, however, such things are the exception. Occasionally you wonder why the person who was taken advantage of allowed themselves to be. There is a saying about things which seem too good to be true, and it's especially applicable in the market. Stockbrokers also get a lot of blame for poorly performing portfolios. While much of this is probably deserved, those who simply turn their money over to a salesman and hope for the best are at least partly to blame. You should hire a true financial advisor with the same care you would take in hiring a doctor to treat you. Become involved in your own portfolio.

Ignorance is a common excuse for losses in the market, but those who use it were often just unwilling to invest their time along with their money. I firmly believe that most individual investors do not do well in the market because: 1) they do not understand it, 2) they fail to plan, and as a result, 3) they behave emotionally.

You can be incredibly informed and still commit all of these errors. Today's individual investor has unprecedented access to information via the internet, the news media, and a rapidly multiplying herd of financial gurus and advisors that are all riding the bull market's wave. Yet, having up to the second quotes and news can be a handicap if not used correctly. Information does not necessarily equal understanding. I cannot emphasize this enough—I have clients who are aware of every development at the companies which they have invested in and try to invest according to the latest news they have read. They are usually not very successful investors, because in most cases the latest news is not what determines the long term prospects of a company. Management, product development, and marketing are the keys to a company's success. So someone buying on "good" short term news and selling on "bad" news often simply ends up buying at the high and selling at the low.

Unfortunately, even professionals who can explain the market's moves may not be much better, at least in terms of translating information into positive results. Wall Street has mastered the art of explaining why the market acted as it did. Note the past tense. If a client asks me why the market went down in a given week, I will probably have a very accurate and reasonable explanation, such as economic action, world events, bond market fluctuations, earnings reports, et cetera. There is always a reason that can be identified for moves in the market, but that doesn't mean that the reason truly explains why the market moved.

My favorite explanation came on a well known financial television program. The commentator asked his guest analyst why a widely held stock and the broader markets had fallen that day without any major economic data or news to explain it. The analyst looked thoughtful and then explained, "Well, it's really quite simple. There were obviously more sellers than buyers, which makes stocks go down, and when more stocks go down than up it makes the averages fall." The commentator nodded intelligently and moved on to the other important news of the day, having enlightened us all while telling us nothing but the obvious.

It is an investment professional's job to stay on top of the market. If we can't figure out why a given event in the market occurred, it is widely known that Wall Street is full of smart and creative people who will think something up that sounds intelligent. I am being partially facetious, but it is my strong opinion that intelligence and advanced degrees don't count for as much as you might think in the long term performance of investment portfolios.

The key to success is not being smarter than the next investor—I can assure you, some of the most successful people I know in the business are not the brightest bulbs. In some cases, that is the key to their success—blind, if not dumb, faith in the plan they set out for themselves. Instead of trying to outsmart the market, they find a discipline that works and stick to it through the ups and downs. By their own admission they do not understand those ups and downs, and thus they ignore them. Adherence to a system and a working discipline will be successful if it is based on a sound basic philosophy. So the key to success as an investor is not necessarily brains, though an IQ north of your latitude is generally useful in most major investment decisions.

To create and be successful with your investment plan, you must have information. I do not mean inside information or hot tips or once in a lifetime opportunities that no one else knows about. I mean knowing what tools you have at your disposal and exercising discipline in using them. This book will hopefully give you a few more of these tools to add to your tool chest.

Why Did You Buy This Book?

1

Why did you buy this book? Probably because you are scared of your greed. You want to experience the historically superior returns of the stock market, but are afraid that you might experience a loss during your attempt to do so. It is often claimed that fear and greed drive the markets, and to a large degree this is true in the short term. If man could make those two emotions get along, maybe then we would continually improve our gains in the market.

The markets are fascinating animals because no one truly understands why they behave as they do. They scare us, occasionally even biting the very hands that feed them. For some, being scared is thrilling, like a dangerous game of hunting. They want to skin the animal, get rich from the fur, and gorge themselves on the meat. The risk of being clawed by the animal only adds to the attraction. Greed, fear, and the possibility of conquest attract us. At least that's what the movies and TV tell us. In reality, many, if not most, individual investors get caught and mauled by this animal from time to time over their investing lives.

Does this mean that we should avoid the market? Certainly not. There is an undeniable case for investing. For most of us, the markets are a way to hopefully provide for a standard of living which is becoming increasingly difficult to maintain. The cost of the American Dream is rising.

The Consumer Price Index (CPI) is a measure of consumer prices over time. The index is calculated on a fixed market basket of goods and services, including shelter, clothing, food, fuels, transportation, medical services, drugs, CDs, money market funds, and others. Now the bad news—the CPI was calculated to be 32.9 in 1966. By the end of 1996, it had risen to 158.6, for an annual simple inflation rate of around 4.2%.

Currently we are in a very low inflation environment, but that may not always be the case. The case for the market boils down to this: rates of return that we can earn on investments which are perceived to be low risk (bank savings accounts, et cetera) simply will not secure our future, so they are in reality an exceptionally high risk in terms of the effect they will have on our lifestyle.

Without examining the onerous problems facing our Social Security and other programs in detail, I think it is accurate to say that most people would agree that our social safety net is on a collision course with demographic fact. There is an accident waiting to happen when the baby boomers, who have created and driven an unprecedented economic and technological expansion, decide that it's time to retire. Some will have the foresight to buckle their financial seatbelts at the beginning of the trip, and will walk away bruised and scratched, but generally all right. Others will not be so lucky. So, unless you want to see your lifestyle erode, the perceived risk of the stock market is a necessary part of your investing life.

Before we go on, let me disclose some things which are important for you to know. First, a little about who I am and why I am writing this now. I have only a few gray hairs at my age, and thus have not experienced a prolonged bear market like we last saw in the early seventies in stocks and the early eighties in bonds. However, in the time that I have worked as a trader, broker, and banker, I have seen quite a few hiccups and even some pretty serious indigestion in the markets. I have traded over a billion dollars of stocks, bonds, and other investments, and learned volumes by sitting with some of the most impressive professionals that I will ever know.

This book is a compilation of my experience, textbook reading, and the knowledge passed to me by these colleagues, some of whom have seen bears larger than the last few generations can imagine. Seeing gains and losses with real money tends to make an impression as to what works and what doesn't.

What sometimes concerns me is that these phenomena we call the markets are currently populated and driven by traders, brokers, investment bankers, analysts, reporters, and investors who have lived through a whole lot less than I. How today's investor reacts to any sort of protracted downturn remains to be seen.

In light of recent market action, many people would consider any correction of longer than a few weeks a bear, since we have not experienced such a thing in so many years. Despite many very convincing reasons that indicate that the bull may have far to run, the fact is that the markets occasionally take breathers. Many of today's market participants have never seen one, except those seemingly insignificant jogs on a graph showing the steady advance of the market for the past century or so. I frequently hear from investors something like this, "Sure, there are those occasional jiggles in the line, but it's obvious that every time that happens the market just goes up again and it turned out to be a great time to buy."

What they forget to add is that it was a great time to buy—in retrospect. I have heard many people say such things, only to watch them panic and sell at precisely the wrong moment. We love instant gratification. A little discomfort or the perception that we have lost money is not gratifying, and thus we act emotionally, often at a loss.

Greed motivates many individual investors to get into the market, often after much of the gains have occurred. Time and time again a client tells me things like, "Look at Company ABC—the stock has quadrupled! Why would I want to buy this XYZ company you are recommending? Its stock has gone down. ABC is going up!"

So, the client buys ABC because he sees all the money other people have made in it. This is greed. One month later it has gone down 30% for no fundamental reason, and the client panics and sells it at a loss. This is fear. Two years later ABC's stock has regained its momentum, and has doubled from the client's purchase price—had he held it. This is the reason that the average individual investor vastly underperforms the broad market. More on this later. For now, suffice it to say that greed, recognized or not, is what motivates most people to invest, but fear forces them out of the market at precisely the worst time.

So, GREED+FEAR=LOSS. Now, if we could just figure out a way to subtract the fear from the equation, we'd all be rich, right? Well, here's how:

$\lambda\chi 3\beta = \Phi$ (\$)
where
β: Greed
λ: Fear
χ: The Unknown

Okay, I'll admit it. This formula doesn't work. As a matter of fact, my two year old helped type it. No formula or trading strategy purporting to magically solve the puzzles of the market does. The market is made up of human beings who exhibit the very same emotional characteristics that we're trying to insulate ourselves from with all the math. Can you quantify human emotion with a system or equation?

People seem to inherently choose the investment alternatives which appeal to their psychological needs. These alternatives are not necessarily those which offer the maximum overall potential.

You can't remove fear from the equation—nobody has ever stolen second base while keeping one foot on first. However, you can manage risk better than you think and create strategies which will make fear less relevant. That is what this book is about. However, first let's establish some basics, without which the best laid plans are useless.

The Basics

2

I am often asked how someone should go about trying to understand the market's ups and downs. An average day in the modern stock market could be described something like this, with some variations:

> *"On Wall Street today, news of lower interest rates sent the stock market up, but then the expectation that these rates would be inflationary sent the market down in profit taking. However, the realization that lower interest rates might stimulate the sluggish economy pushed the market up in short covering, before it ultimately went down due to program selling sparked by fears that an overheated economy would lead to a re-imposition of higher interest rates."*

Confusing? Of course. We cannot truly explain the short term swings of the markets, no matter how much jargon is used. Yet for many people, the traditional method of avoiding risk is to try to do what we call "timing" the market, in which the investor attempts to buy at the bottom and sell at the peak. This type of thinking is pervasive in the market for reasons we've already discussed. It is also counterproductive to your portfolio's success. This doesn't mean that you should not adjust certain aspects of your portfolio due to changing market conditions, but simply that there should be no such thing as being "out" of the market in a long term investment portfolio.

Though I can always find someone to argue that they really can time the market, I have yet to find anyone who can show real evidence over more than one or two market turns. Maybe someday I'll meet someone who can convince me. I would be curious about their methodology, but it wouldn't change how I do things. Timing the market is at best a waste of time and at worst, damaging to your long term results.

In mid July, 1996, I received a somewhat alarming piece of junk mail from a well known market analyst who has long claimed to have "called every market crash in the last two decades"—all one of them. The front of this letter said, "Sell all your U.S. stocks right now!" I know of several major account holders who listened to this particular analyst and sold everything. This "market call" to sell and go to all cash was made when the Dow had dropped 4.6% since its high in May. The Dow subsequently gained 17% to close 1996 at 6,448.27. It is currently up over 23% year-to-date, excluding dividends. I understand that this same analyst became bullish on the market a few months ago, so maybe she is back in the market and only missed out on gains of 30% or so, instead of the 40% that the market is up since the time she said to "sell all your U.S. stocks right now!"

In all fairness to this and other prognosticators, I am looking at this period of time with the benefit of hindsight. However, the common saying that "money is made by time in the market, not timing the market" is true. You cannot time the market. Since 1965, if you had put $1,000 into the S&P 500 at exactly the "best" (at the lowest price point of that year) your return would have been 11.7% per year. While this seems low in light of the recent market moves, it is actually a return that is very respectable in historical terms. The ability to put your money into the market at exactly its lowest point each year would be impressive. It is also impossible.

Fortunately, there is hope even for us dummies who can't time the market perfectly to the exact day. Let's return to 1965. If you had simply left instructions to invest $1,000 into the market on the first trading day of every year, then left for a 30 year vacation, you would find that your average annual return when you came back in 1995 was about 11.0% per year. Not bad, considering that your completely uninformed investing made almost as much as the unlikely scenario of the perfect timer.

But what if you are an inherently unlucky person who has a knack for paying too much for everything? Let's go back to the above scenario. Assume that in every year since 1965, you have managed, through a curse that seems unique to you, to put your $1,000 into the market at the exact high point of the market every single year. Not to worry—if you had just left the investments alone, you would still have averaged more than 10.5% per year. As you can see, over time, the difference between market timing and consistent investing becomes very blurred. Time in the market is the key, not timing the market.

When I am speaking to groups there is invariably someone who challenges my assertions that buy and hold strategies really work better than timing the market. I like to ask that person to tell me just what day, what week, what month, or even which year the current bull market will end. In 1994 I often heard the answer "mid year 1995" yet, as I am writing this, the Dow has doubled in under three years. Those who have stayed in for the whole ride since that time might still be profitable even if the market sheds 20% or so next month.

How about those who followed their instinct (which I believe is just a more comfortable way to describe emotion) and stayed on the sidelines? Well, they've got the money they started with, plus hopefully 4 or 5% per year if they at least had the foresight to leave it in money market funds and not a bank. They also have the sure knowledge that their standard of living and retirement lifestyle are falling behind, because prices rise to meet demand, and if everyone else has more income there will be more demand. If your assets don't keep pace with others who maintain the same standard of living, you will most likely eventually not share that standard. This is a brutal truth, but worth considering. What is the cost of your fear?

Just to be obnoxious and press this point further, let's say that you invested $100 into the stock market (again, we'll use the S&P 500 index as our "stock market") in 1925. Had you allowed that money to compound, you would now have $137,100. However, had you somehow missed only the 35 best months out of the 852 months through 1996, you would now have only $1,200.50, or less than 1/100th of the value of simply staying invested. This is because the market tends to move rapidly up (and down) in spurts, and unless you can tell exactly when the next move is going to be, it's probably best just to stay invested.

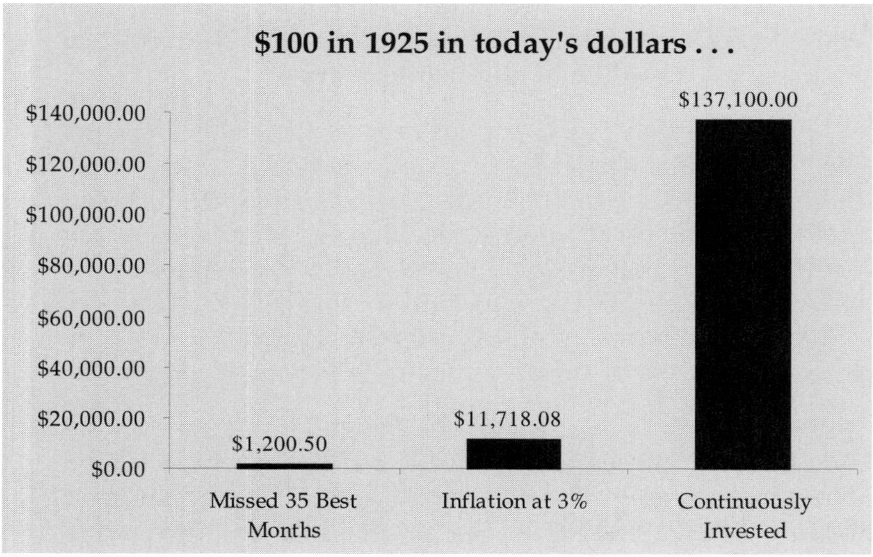

A recent study by Terrance Odean, an economist at the University of California at Davis, finds that the investments made by individuals investors tend to do worse on average than the market averages. Even worse, the stocks that individual investors sell tend to beat the market after they sell them. The conclusion of the study was that small investors seem to have a propensity to sell their winners early and hold onto losers too long.

A similar study was done by one of the major U.S. brokerage firms and Lipper Analytical Services in 1994. It concluded that the average investor in the 30 largest balanced mutual funds made an average annual return of 6.2% between 1980 and 1994, while the actual annualized performance of those funds was over 9.5%.

Why did all these investors make 1/3 less than they should have? Emotion. People have a distinct talent for buying because they see the market (or an individual stock) going up and selling because they see it going down. Common sense, of course, dictates the precise opposite strategy, and historical returns make it evident that it actually makes the most sense to simply stay in the market, dollar cost average, and compound your money.

Why do we act the way we do, when common sense points us the right way? There is a well known example that illustrates our natural tendencies to act differently when we are facing a gain versus when we are facing a loss. Amos Tversky of Stanford University and Daniel Kahneman of Princeton University used tests of this theory. First, they asked people to choose between 1) a certain gain of $800, or 2) an opportunity that has an 85% chance of returning $1,000 and a 15% chance of earning nothing.

Though there were gains possible in both options, most people chose number one (a guaranteed $800) despite the fact that, mathematically, option two was more desirable. This is because if the exercise is repeated over and over (as we make many successive investment decisions), an 85% chance of earning $1,000 yields an expectation of $850 on average. A 100% chance of earning $800 gives the expected $800 each time. Pure mathematics says that those who choose option two consistently would be more profitable, even though occasionally they would get nothing.

The interesting part of the study came when the possibilities were reversed. Tversky and Kahneman asked their research group to choose between 1) a certain loss of $800, or 2) an 85% chance of losing $1,000 and a 15% chance of losing nothing. This time, a large majority of the subjects chose option two, though in this case that was the least attractive option. 85% of the time, those consistently choosing option two would lose $1,000, for an average loss of $850. Option one would give a loss of $800 every time, which on average is more preferable than an average loss of $850.

It is an interesting exercise to honestly answer the above questions. It has been my experience that most of us behave this way unless we pause to examine our decisions objectively. In managing our money, this frequently causes investors to sell their best holdings too soon, and hang on to underperforming investments too long. It also causes the average investor to sell at market bottoms and buy at market tops, which greatly hampers results.

So the best way to invest is to put your money in the market and leave it there regardless of what seems to be happening, right? Well, the simple answer is yes, because we cannot predict all the millions of forces that may make the market move in seemingly irrational directions. We trust the basic premise that the growth of the economy over years and decades will compound our assets handsomely, as they have in any 20-year period regardless of when you started since the market has existed.

However, that is much harder to do in practice than to say when you're discussing investments during a bull market. So how do you sleep at night and still stay in the market?

Solid Foundations

3

Before beginning a discussion of hedging and to expose any biases I have, I should share my fundamental investment philosophy. Simply put, your goal should be to compound your investment capital at the maximum rate of return that is consistent with the risk you are willing to accept. Since stocks have undeniably been the best performing asset class, I recommend a healthy dose of stocks in most portfolios unless a client wants so called "riskless" investments only.

To make the reason for this clear, here are the annual compounded rates of return from 1926 through 1996, with an illustration of what $1,000 invested would be worth today:

	Annual Rate of Return (ROR)	$1,000 Invested 1926 through 1996
Small company stocks	12.40%	$2,884,687
Large company stocks	10.70%	1,149,732
Long term government bonds	5.10%	61,810
Treasury bills	3.70%	31,678
Inflation rate	3.12%	24,328

These numbers are impressive, especially when you note how large a difference there is over time. Time in the market at a consistent rate of return can seemingly do miracles. Despite economic recessions and depressions, market crashes, wars, and thousands of theories claiming to create instant wealth, high quality (large company) stocks have given us almost 19 times the return of government bonds, 36 times treasury bills, and over 47 times inflation.

However, few of us were around in 1926, so are examples like this relevant? Certainly. To prove it, let's look at just the last ten years.

	Annual Rate of Return (ROR)	$1,000 Invested 1986 through 1996
Small company stocks	19.50%	$2,533
Large company stocks	13.95%	1,929
Long term government bonds	5.50%	1,288
Treasury bills	4.80%	1,246

At the very beginning of the decade shown here (1986 to 1996) there was a market crash, in October, 1987. Even so, small company stocks returned 97% more than bonds, and 103% more than the average money market fund.

These numbers become even more telling when the real effects of inflation and taxes are included. Assuming inflation of 3% and income taxes of 28%, we would have realized "real" growth of our money as follows:

	Annual Rate of Return (ROR)	$1,000 Invested 1986 - 1996	Effects of Taxes	Effect of Inflation	Real ROR
Small Company Stocks	19.50%	$2,533	-285.13	-146.39	11.01%
Large Company Stocks	13.95%	1,929	-195.39	-146.39	5.87%
Government Bonds	5.50%	1,288	-72.22	-146.39	0.69%
Money Market Average	4.80%	1,246	-62.70	-146.39	0.37%

As you can see, it's hard to argue against the stock market.

Okay, so there is a great case for stocks. But there's more to do than just buy stocks. You must have a philosophy or discipline to guide you.

Personally, I am a long term fundamental investor. I know many so called investors who seek only to make the most money possible by next week yet have no real conception of what risk they are taking. (Remember, if you are up 80% one year and down "only" 50% the next, you still lose 10% of your money!) Those who are wise enough to take the long view of the market and allocate their assets accordingly will be wealthy at the end. Does it really matter who is ahead halfway through the race, or who wins?

Good companies do not change to any great extent from day to day or sometimes even year to year. However, investors' perceptions can fluctuate dramatically in only an hour. When a good company temporarily falls from favor, there may be an opportunity to become an owner of its stocks or bonds at a lower price. Providing that the long term fundamentals of the company remain intact, the lower price will provide the patient investor with a superior return. Over the long term a company's earnings and management will drive the price of a stock and reflect its true economic value.

There are some attributes that I have noticed many successful investors have in common. They seldom stray far from the following basics.

Be patient. Making money is a slow process—though you always hear about it, instant gratification is rare, and you must tolerate pain to profit. Sometimes you need to hold a stock for two to three years before expecting results.

Ignore market noise. The market can have a short term impact on the price of a stock. If the company is a good investment, pay attention to the company and not the external factors which temporarily drive its price. Also remember that historically the market has always gone up, and that the best time to buy is when emotional investors overreact and sell a fundamentally good company.

Watch your emotions. Emotions should have no place in investment decisions. Fear and greed truly drive the market. Remain objective; avoid fads, personal prejudice, and media hype. If the fundamentals of a company have changed, don't let an emotional attachment affect the decision.

Don't follow the crowd. The media, and unfortunately some investment professionals, tend to overstate both the good and the bad news. This can dramatically influence price in the short term. Take advantage of the optimistic and pessimistic extremes which are so often displayed in the market, but don't follow them.

Taxes are an issue. Though taxes may be a large factor in your overall investment plan, don't let them be the sole reason for an investment decision. Ignoring the fundamentals to get more favorable tax treatment in the future could create a significant loss.

Have realistic expectations. Don't expect to make 30% or more from your core investments year after year. Even the greatest investors in history—Buffet, Lynch, and others—have not sustained that kind of performance over the long term. My experience suggests that "brilliant" investors are often the beneficiaries of luck, ethical lapses, or more recently an unprecedented bull market. I've hit some financial home runs before, but I don't expect to all the time. The long term returns on stocks have been around 10 to 12% per year, recent performance notwithstanding. If you can add 5% or more to the market averages you're doing unusually well.

Admit mistakes. By cutting a loser quickly, you avoid big losses. If the fundamentals have deteriorated you may be better off taking a loss and reinvesting your capital in something more productive. Ride the strongest horse you can find instead of trying to whip a tired one into going faster.

These seem like common sense statements, but I am continually surprised how often investors—and investment professionals—violate them. Your portfolio must be built with discipline; otherwise, the remaining chapters of this book will serve only to give you the knowledge to avoid some short term losses, but will probably not improve your long term rate of return.

So, what should you put in your portfolio? Every investor has his or her own method for selecting an equity, some more complicated than others. This is a process we should all go through before selecting any investment. Ask yourself, "Why should I own this?" Again, I have seen commonalities that seem to be present in the most successful investors' portfolios. Some examples of what to look for in an investment are:

Buy companies, not stocks. Do not buy a stock price. Remember that a share of stock is simply a piece of the company, its products, and its management. Find out about the management, since they are the people who will sell existing products, develop new ones, and hopefully create value for you as a shareholder. When you buy stock, you are essentially hiring these people to manage your money.

Be alert to a relatively low Price to Earnings (PE) multiple. If the PE ratio is below those of similar companies and less than the company's long term growth rate, the stock may be undervalued. Also, a history of predictable earnings growth is a positive factor. One of the companies that I own has turned in record earnings and revenues for 50 years in a row!

Check for the probability of success. I look for several viable reasons that a company will be successful for every point of perceived downside risk.

Look for Book Value (BV) or Net Asset Value (NAV). If you buy a company near or below its liquidation value it can sometimes provide a measure of downside protection.

Focus on low debt, high cash flow, and clean balance sheets. A highly leveraged company is not as flexible to develop new products, expand, or make acquisitions as one with open credit and cash on hand. Though some industries are normally more leveraged than others, I typically avoid a debt to equity ratio in excess of 50%.

What about strong franchises? With a few exceptions (though I do make them), stay away from stocks which have incredible concepts, but no earnings. It is difficult to tell the difference between a fad, a trend, and a future paradigm. Wait until the earnings are apparent, and you will know what has become the standard.

Turnaround stories can make a profit. If the fundamentals of a company are intact or improving, take advantage of negative market psychology when a company is trading near its 52 week low. This strategy can take some time, but can provide handsome returns.

Cash in on dividends. Attractive dividends are a great reason to buy some stocks if the company is generating enough cash over the long term to support the dividend being paid. I also look for a history of dividend growth and predictability. Dividends are great to have around when the markets are bearish!

Consider price averaging. A company's price sometimes is not at all reflective of its value. If the price falls after you buy it and the fundamentals are still intact, consider adding to the position to lower your cost basis.

There are other things worth your consideration. Insider buying, technical analysis, and general economic, monetary, and market trends can also be part of a decision to invest in a security, depending on your own style. It is always important to see the "big picture."

This is overly simplistic, and does not cover the basic needs for diversification, asset allocation, and other aspects of portfolio management. A full discussion of these topics is not the purpose of this book, but I do recommend that beginning investors become familiar with them if they are not already. There are dozens of excellent sources in this area. A few that I have found to be helpful to some of my clients are *Stocks for the Long Run* by Jeremy J. Siegel, the classic *The Intelligent Investor* by Benjamin Graham, and for an admittedly opinionated but usually educational view, *How to Make Money in Stocks* by William O'Neil. *The A to Z of Wall Street* by Sandra S. Hildreth or a good dictionary of finance and investment terms is valuable to have on hand as well. I cannot emphasize how important a basically sound portfolio is to your long term success, so take the time to build one the right way.

Defensive Investing

4

Defensive investing does not mean timing the market. It does mean positioning your investments to not only do well in good markets, but also to do comparatively well in down markets. Does this mean that you will be making money while the market goes down? Possibly, but not necessarily. "Comparatively well" may mean that your investments temporarily fall but not to the same degree as the broad markets, or that they are more resilient in their return to original levels. I maintain that outperforming the market on the way down is just as important to long term results as doing better than the averages when the markets are on the way up.

So, the market is flying high, and you own the stocks that took off. While you are enjoying their heights, you wonder if there wouldn't be something that might not require an oxygen mask to own. If you assume that the underlying companies (and the broad economy over the long term cycle) are intact and operating with the fundamental story you originally bought, how should you invest to outperform the market in a downturn?

Asset allocation

Before you take any other factor into consideration in building a defensive portfolio, figure out what your asset allocation is. Several studies have suggested that asset allocation determines the majority of a portfolio's return. My experience confirms this. If you are in the right market, the right country, or the right sector it becomes incredibly easy to make money. Unfortunately, the converse is also true.

Asset allocation is the first step in creating a true portfolio, instead of an account filled with unrelated stocks, bonds, funds, or other securities. The classic concept of asset allocation is expressed as a percentage devoted to certain security types, normally defined as stocks, bonds, and cash. So, if your allocation is 50/40/10, you own 50% stocks, 40% bonds, and 10% cash or money market funds.

Sample Asset Allocation

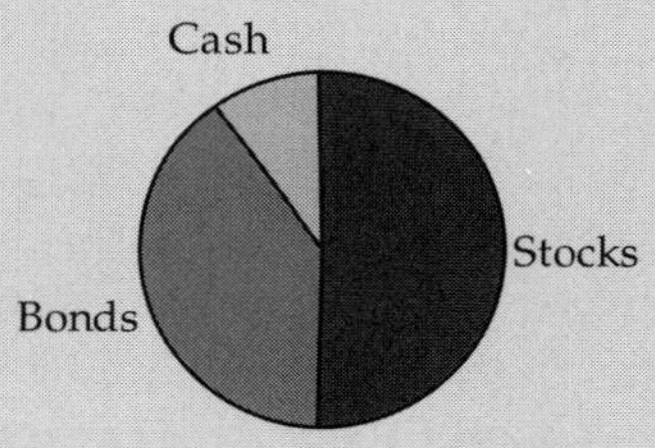

Most of the large brokerages maintain a recommended allocation which they change from time to time according to their views of the markets. When they believe that the stock market may provide a lower return than bonds in the intermediate term, they may change the allocation to own more bonds and fewer stocks.

However, it is wise not to get caught up in tinkering with your allocation too frequently. Force yourself to focus on the portfolio instead of each individual investment. If a given investment is not behaving properly within your portfolio, then by all means get rid of it. The key word here is "behaving." Most people consider an investment to be behaving properly only if it is in the process of going up, but that may not be the most profitable way to manage your portfolio.

If you are looking at your whole portfolio, not just one investment, you will hopefully have stocks, bonds, and other investments that are expected to behave differently in the same market conditions. Put another way, you don't want every security in your portfolio to go up or down at exactly the same time, or the volatility inherent in certain investments may leave a big, frightening bear footprint in the middle of your portfolio from time to time. It's acceptable for one stock to seem dormant or even fall a little if that is what you would expect from it in a given market, even while other components of the portfolio rise aggressively when faced with the same market conditions.

A very general example of this can be found by comparing "growth" stocks to "value" stocks. Growth stocks are those which have exhibited faster than average earnings gains and are expected to continue to do so in the future. Investing in growth stocks can often give you an above average return over time, but they can be riskier than the average stock because they usually sport higher price to earnings ratios and make little or no dividend payments. Value stocks are ones that look undervalued compared to other companies in its sector, or is part of a market sector that looks cheap versus the broad market. Relative value may be measured in many ways: a low price to earnings ratio, a comparably high dividend yield, attractive book value, et cetera. Historically, we see periods of time in which the philosophy of growth investing outperforms value investing, then vice versa as investors become defensive and buy companies which they think offer good value. Value stocks are normally expected to perform better in downturns because they are already "cheap" compared to the broad market.

Because of this, I believe it is wise to mix a little of each style of investing (value and growth) into a portfolio. It is difficult if not impossible to predict when growth will outperform value and vice versa. Both styles may do well in bull markets and may fall in bear markets, but to differing degrees. More detailed descriptions of these and other classes of stock holdings are coming up in this chapter.

Some market professionals go so far to separate the two styles of investing into distinct asset classes, and identify a recommended allocation which includes a value versus growth component:

Sample Asset Allocation Including Growth Value Stock

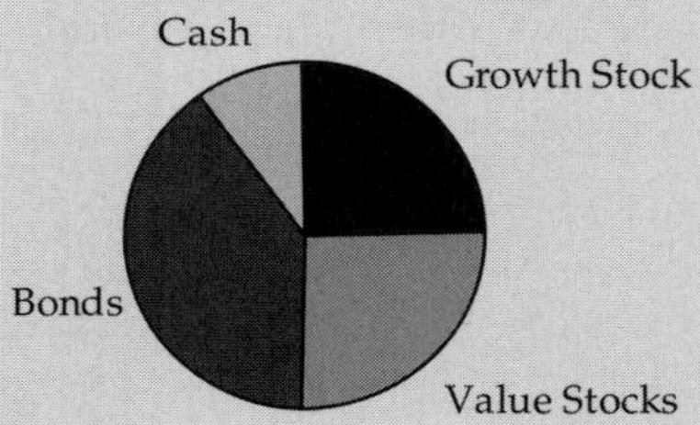

Aside from growth versus value, there are many subdivisions within stocks that you should know about. Though I cannot cover them all, let's get some very basic definitions in place, so we can then discuss what asset allocation may be appropriate for your investment goals.

Cash can be defined as security that is equivalent to cash and has little if any risk or loss of capital or fluctuation in price, such as money market funds, bank savings accounts, short term (three months or less) bonds, et cetera.

Growth stocks, as we discussed earlier, are companies which may be younger and more agile than larger companies. Often, they have a new product or strategy that is unique and may even create a new industry segment. For instance, semiconductors, software, new restaurant concepts, and many other types of companies may exhibit rapid growth. They may be able to add 50% or even more to the revenues and earnings for several years running, and often trade at higher valuations due to positive expectations for the future. Growth stocks tend to be more volatile and pay no dividends, but if well selected can multiply your money faster than almost any other asset class. The key is figuring out what the next growth industry will be, and which company will create and/or dominate that industry.

When an industry, company, or entire economic region is out of favor with investors, certain stocks may become "cheap" compared to other stocks in the market. These are called value stocks. For example, if steel prices suddenly drop, the stocks of steel makers may become depressed as well. If an investor thinks that the drop is temporary and the stocks will rise in value as soon as steel prices recover, she may decide that steel stocks are good value compared to other market sectors. Deciding what is good value is much like shopping at a store. When you are deciding which product to buy, you look at price versus what the product offers in terms of quality, features, and volume. The product which has the most for the least money is probably what you will select. If a stock has fallen more than is justified given the fundamentals of its business, it is "on sale" and could be a good buy for the informed shopper.

Blue Chips is the traditional name for the large, well established companies with broad name recognition and a long history of earnings and oftentimes, dividends. Though some investment professionals (including me) would disagree, the term is usually applied primarily to stocks on the New York Stock Exchange. Examples are companies such as General Electric, Chevron, JP Morgan, Philip Morris, Boeing, McDonald's, et cetera. Just because a company is a blue chip does not mean that it will not rise and fall like any other stock. As a matter of fact, the Dow Jones Industrial Average is comprised of thirty stocks that are considered "the" blue chips, and that index is certainly subject to volatility.

A well selected group of blue chip stocks can provide a stable core to a portfolio. However, remember that most of these companies were at one time very young, aggressive growth companies. There are growth companies today which may be on the verge of becoming tomorrow's blue chips. Big Macs, light bulbs, microwaves, gas stations, and giant jet airplanes are commonplace today, but they were revolutionary not so very long ago. Cellular telephones, computers, ATM machines, and grocery checkout scanners are fairly recent innovations, but multibillion dollar companies have grown around them. The products which are pervasive in our everyday lives are often the ones which will create future blue chip companies.

International investing, though not for the faint of heart, can be very rewarding and can provide an excellent hedge against turmoil in U.S. markets. When currencies begin to strengthen versus the U.S. dollar, investments in those countries may rise in U.S. dollar terms even though they may not be doing much in local currency. In light of recent history many investors will avoid international markets, which I believe may be a mistake in retrospect. The key is purchasing high quality holdings, either via a good quality global mutual fund or actually buying the "blue chip" of a given country. For instance, Toyota or Sony in Japan, Ericsson in Sweden, and Volkswagen in Germany, are all globally recognized companies. Also, there can occasionally be value in looking at the companies which provide services that are basic in most developed countries—telephone, electricity, natural gas, and similar industries. I should note that to invest directly in international stocks demands a great deal of research, knowledge, ongoing access to information, and sometimes much higher transaction costs. For most investors, I prefer to use mutual funds, unit trusts (baskets of stock selected by analysts), or derivative securities (see the chapter entitled "Bored

MBAs") to participate in international markets. However, if you are up to the challenge I believe that you can be well compensated for the risk over time.

Many types of investments fall into the speculative securities category. I will not spend a lot of time on them, except to say that they belong only in very aggressive, risk tolerant portfolios. So called "penny" (low priced) stocks, some types of options and futures trading, some initial public offerings, and various other investments could qualify for this label. Generally, where the potential gain is huge but the potential loss could be large as well, the security could be considered speculative. Though speculation has its place as a small part of an overall portfolio, remember that if the potential return is incredible, the risk is usually extremely high as well.

Though we'll discuss the basics of bonds further in future chapters, for now I will note that the word "bond" is an incredibly broad definition that covers a market three times the size of the stock market in terms of dollar volume transacted. Bonds are essentially loans made by investors to the issuers of the bonds. The U. S. and foreign governments, federal agencies, corporations, banks, municipalities, states, and almost every other imaginable entity has or will issue bonds of some type. There are also many "hybrid" securities, which include aspects of a bond but can move in direct relation to the company's stock price as well.

In my opinion, few people truly understand bonds, yet the bond market has a huge effect on the stockmarket and the very fundamentals of the economy. Though the chapter on "Fixed Returns" may help with a basic understanding of the mechanics of bonds, I would recommend further reading on the subject for investors who want to understand the market in depth. The standard of the industry in my opinion is the *Handbook of Fixed Income Securities,* by Franklin Fabozzi. It is very technical, but also has excellent references to other sources. I also recommend *How the Bond Market Works,* published by the New York Institute of Finance.

Proper asset allocation will focus more on your investment goals than current market conditions. However, understanding how various types of securities might behave given certain market conditions is crucial.

Determining your own asset allocation

Not all investors should have the same asset allocations, of course. For instance, if you have many years until retirement and can afford to absorb the potential loss of some principal, you may be better off with a heavy weighting in stocks. Though stocks have undeniably been more volatile than bonds or money market funds, they have also provided a far better return over time. As long as you have time to recover from the losses that are possible over the short term in the stock market, you are probably better off investing more aggressively. That way, you have a greater potential to grow your assets in the long term.

For an investor who is earning a good income and is at least thirty years from retirement, I might recommend a portfolio somewhat like this:

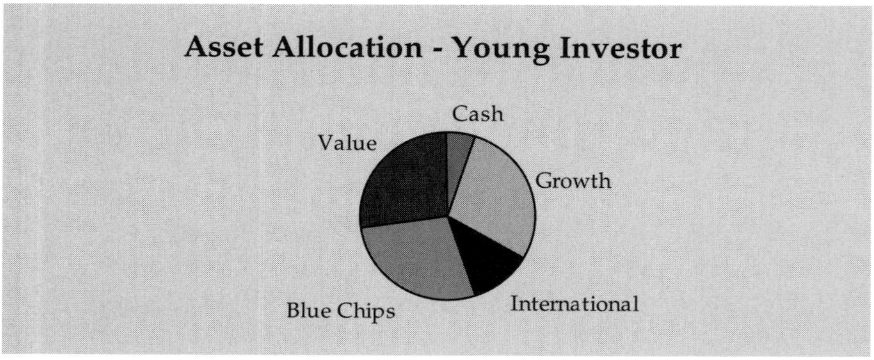

At mid life, however, most investors begin thinking about how close they are getting to retirement, and want to make some changes to secure what they already have. This may involve a gradual move into bonds and increasing the stability of the stock holdings by adding to the large capitalization blue chip positions. (Hopefully, some of the growth stocks purchased decades before have matured into near blue-chip status, and the value stocks didn't stay cheap after you bought them.) At age fifty I would normally advise an investor to structure a portfolio with an increasingly predictable rate of return. This may take the form of a growing bond component (to provide for a fixed rate of return) and more blue chip stocks (which traditionally pay larger dividends than other stocks and have more stable businesses).

Asset Allocation - Mid Life

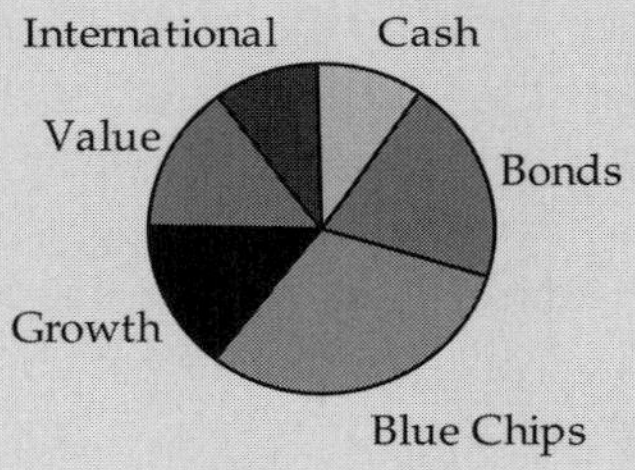

As you move closer to retirement, it may be appropriate to decrease some of the stock holdings even more. However, when possible I try to maintain at least some stock holdings, albeit high quality ones, in a retired investor's portfolio. If the portfolio has more principal than is necessary to generate the income needed by the investor, it makes sense to try to grow the principal as well to increase the standard of living, leave more to heirs, or simply increase the "margin of safety" in case the investor lives to 100. With ever increasing life spans, many people are outliving their savings. Growth should always be an investment goal, even if it eventually becomes subordinated to the generation of income and safety of principal.

Unfortunately, many people reading this did not start investing at age thirty, and now may be approaching retirement without the idealized portfolio and ongoing investment I have described above.

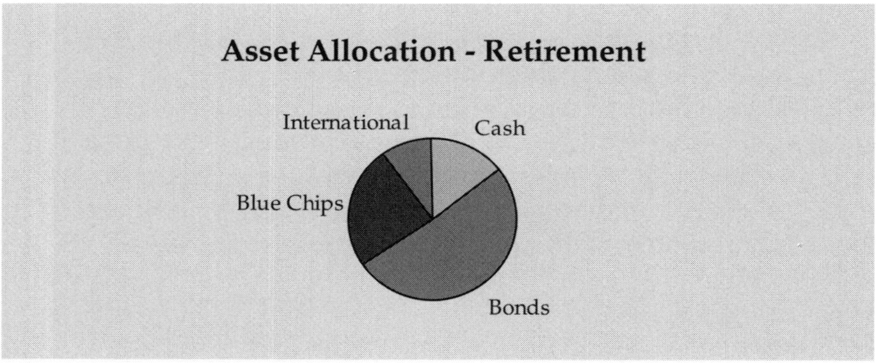

If this describes you, what should you do? Start right now. The key is getting principal established, grown, and protected. Keep in mind that taking foolish risks does not serve you well at any time in your investing life. Be aggressive with decreasing portions of your portfolio as you approach retirement, but do take prudent risks if that is what you must do to obtain the returns you need to fund your goals.

The remainder of this chapter will cover some concepts that are good to be aware of while building your portfolio: Modern Portfolio Theory (MPT), diversification, and defensive industries.

Modern Portfolio Theory (MPT) and commodities

In 1990 the Nobel Prize in Economics was awarded to the developers of an investment study known as Modern Portfolio Theory (MPT). This concept has gained many advocates in the last few years, for both its observations on the behavior of the markets and the discipline it brings to a portfolio when those observations are applied.

Basically, MPT's premise is that strictly defined classes of assets will behave differently at different times, and that by investing across certain asset classes, above average returns can be attained with lower risk over time. The crux of the study (and many subsequent ones) was that more than 95% of a portfolio's return is determined by asset allocation, not stock picking or market timing. It follows that the things that most investors worry the most about—picking a specific stock, buying it at its low point, and getting the lowest commission on the trade—are really not all that relevant to the end results of the portfolio over time. Selection of asset class (stocks, bonds, commodities, et cetera), subclasses (value versus growth stocks, Treasury versus corporate bonds, agricultural versus precious metal futures), and sectors (blue chip versus small capitalization stocks, investment grade versus junk bonds, gold versus platinum futures) are far more important than the things that we spend most of our time on in managing a portfolio.

The interesting part of MPT is what it says about human nature and our tendency to underperform the market. For example, let's say that small cap growth stocks are doing very well, and large cap value stocks have been languishing for a few years. Most investors would sell their large caps and buy the small caps based on this, because the small caps have been performing well. Note the past tense—"have been performing." This common behavior assures that an overwhelming majority of investors will underperform the broad markets. Why? When you buy last year's best performing asset class (or worse, last year's best performing mutual fund or stock), you are buying an asset which has already experienced a period of appreciation. It is likely that it may not continue to outperform as other asset types come into favor.

Does this mean that you should buy whatever went down the most last year? No. MPT advocates a more passive approach, in which precisely defined asset classes are used for allocation within a portfolio. Very few changes are made over time if the initial allocation is appropriate for your risk tolerance; by simply tracking (not even beating) the market you will be doing better than 3/4 of the managers and mutual funds.

So, if it's best just to "track the market," why not simply buy index funds or some other type of stock market index security, move to the Bahamas, and forget about it? As you might guess, it's not that simple. The well known indices, such as the Dow Jones Industrial Average, S&P 500, and NASDAQ, contain only stocks, and a limited number of stocks at that. Other asset classes like bonds, commodities, foreign stocks, and variations within those asset classes are not included in these indexes that we consider to be "the market." MPT demonstrates that having portfolio components which include those asset classes can improve return and decreases risk over time, with the degree of improvement increasing over longer periods of time.

Though bonds and other asset classes are covered elsewhere, I have discussed MPT because of its conclusions about the commodities portion of a portfolio. I believe that for most larger portfolios a well managed commodities component can actually reduce risk over time, even though that component may be extremely volatile if held as an investment on its own. This is because there have been periods in which stocks and bonds have been hurt badly by rising inflation and other economic or political events, while physical assets like gold, corn, oil, copper, wheat, and orange juice become much more valuable on a relative basis. Money can also be made by good managers by betting on declines in certain commodity prices. Without entering the arcane world of commodities trading I will simply say that I believe this component is a valuable part of asset allocation.

One of the most popular forms of doing this is commonly termed as a "managed futures" fund. These funds (usually partnerships or other structures) are run by professional commodities firms, who may or may not receive a portion of the profits generated by their fund. They have widely varying levels of cost, volatility, and risk, and generally the risk of loss is limited to the amount of your original investment only. Other people like to use "hard asset" or "natural resources" funds, which may invest in the stocks of companies which stand to benefit by changes in commodity prices, or which may invest in the commodities themselves. This is an area of opportunity if well executed, but use extreme care and make sure you understand exactly the worst case and best case scenarios with which you could be faced before investing any money.

One other note about MPT portfolios in general: because they are often allocated in a more passive manner than most portfolios, there is lower turnover in the portfolio, and hence fewer capital gains and other taxes. This tax efficient investing can make a tremendous difference to your return over time, since at current rates most of us give state and federal governments up to one-third of all our realized gains.

Diversification

Within each asset class there is another important type of allocation which you should be aware of. For the equity (stock) component of your portfolio, you don't want to own companies which are all in the same industry, because that would expose you to a large degree of risk if that industry experienced a slowdown. For instance, even if you believe that technology companies are going to be the best long term stocks to own, you probably should not have all of your funds allocated to that sector. The next section will deal with defensive industries, which can be important tools to diversify a portfolio.

One key aspect of diversification is often overlooked. We have undeniably entered a period in which our economy is increasingly global. Because of this, I believe that wise investors will keep a portion of their assets invested outside of the United States. Some people I know have been hurt by doing so and have vowed to never do so again. This is often due to a poor choice of investment vehicles or taking the wrong exit, even though they may have been on the right highway.

I generally recommend that clients maintain a 10 to 20% international allocation, especially when certain international markets are undervalued relative to the United States. There are many methods by which to own foreign securities—mutual funds, trusts, derivatives, and even buying individual stocks on foreign exchanges or via ADRs (American Depository Receipts, certificates representing foreign stocks but traded on U.S. exchanges). This is a large subject that I can't discuss in detail here. I simply recommend that you make sure that any consultant you work with is well versed in markets outside of the U.S.

Another form of diversification that is not often considered is diversity by exchange. The U.S. stock exchanges can behave very differently, and on average have varying degrees of liquidity, volatility, et cetera. The NASDAQ exchange, for instance, is a negotiated market in which news on a stock can create extreme volatility, with stocks sometimes "gapping" after news is released. This can create opportunity, but can also hurt badly if you're on the wrong side of the market. For instance, even though a stock last traded at $20, it may open at $12 after some bad news is released, with no trades in between—there was no chance to sell at any price between $20 and $12.

Since NASDAQ prices are determined by traders who are trying to make money for themselves as well as executing trades, the market will inherently be more volatile. In the past, a stock could trade at a given price all day without your order at that price being executed. Why? Assume that the stock is quoted $13 7/8 by $14 1/8, meaning that the trader is willing to buy stock from anyone at $13 7/8 and will sell to anyone at $14 1/8. If you enter an order to sell your shares "in the spread" at $14, it is entirely conceivable that you would never get your trade executed until the trader was willing to improve the bid from $13 7/8, even though you may see hundreds of shares trade at $14. Some of the recent changes in NASDAQ will greatly improve this in my opinion, especially the rules which force traders to show a customer's price along with their own and other rules which are designed to narrow spreads.

In contrast, the New York Stock Exchange (NYSE) and American Stock Exchange (ASE) are auction markets, in which buyers and sellers are matched in a specialist's book or via computer. While stocks on these exchanges do occasionally gap, the exchange will generally not begin trading a stock until there are both buyers and sellers at similar price levels. This reduces volatility and can offer liquidity for larger companies. Is this to say that the NYSE or ASE is better than NASDAQ? Not at all. NASDAQ is the source for many of the fastest growing, conceptually exciting companies in our country. It provides an exceptional forum to determine what the true value of a stock is over time. However, in my opinion, the fact that it is a negotiated market may make it more volatile and subject to maneuvering by other investors and traders.

Asset allocation and diversification are basically the processes of ensuring that your portfolio is not overexposed to any one single asset class, market, exchange, industry sector, or individual company. A good allocation is the beginning of a solid portfolio.

Defensive industries

If you are concerned that the economy or a world event will cause your portfolio to fall, you may want to include holdings which normally outperform the market in a negative environment. These holdings will hopefully make up for the losses in the rest of your portfolio in a correction and the time following it, basically making your portfolio less susceptible to short term market fluctuations.

There are certain industry groups which generally do not go down as much as the broad market and recover faster in difficult economic times. Though what is considered a defensive industry varies widely depending on who you are talking to, consider which companies make products which will be purchased to a large degree regardless of what economic conditions exist. The last things people will give up are food, medicine, and other necessities. The first things they give up are the extras that we all like to have but may not need, such as clothes, new cars and houses, consumer electronics, restaurant dining, et cetera.

Some industries may even rise in times that everything else is falling. An easy example of this is the defense sector. The outbreak of fighting is seldom good in the short term for the market, though defense stocks may rise quickly as traders start counting all the new tanks, planes, rockets, and everything else required to conduct battle. Similarly, companies which produce certain commodities like precious metals, oil, and chemicals are attractive when the economy is experiencing rapid price inflation, since they can get higher prices for their products even though their cost of production may remain the same if they already own the mine or oil well.

There is no perfect definition of a defensive industry or company. It is simply wise to consider what the effects of a recession, war, political instability, or other events would be on your portfolio, and invest accordingly.

Contrarian investing

You may see funds or partnerships with stated investment goals that identify them as "contrarian." This means that they will attempt to position themselves to benefit if certain core markets fall. Some of these funds have actually done surprisingly well in the past decade in light of the fact that they've been playing toreador to a very, very big bull market. Whether this is due to the fact that they are not truly contrarian or whether they simply have exceptional management and strategy in all markets is a matter for inquiry.

While this type of fund may seem like an ideal way to hedge your portfolio, a high degree of caution is warranted. Before buying any such investment, find out how the managers think the fund will benefit by a falling market and how much correlation the fund has had to the market in the past. Understand how and why the fund you are considering should perform in a falling market.

To answer these questions, you will need to find out several details about the fund, its investments, and its managers. Do they sell stocks short and actively bet on declines that the market will fall, do they simply invest in defensive industries, or does the fund buy puts to protect a portfolio designed to track an index? This book will hopefully provide a basic understanding of these same concepts, so find a fund which should exhibit the kind of behavior which you want in a certain type of market environment.

Remember that a fund that sells short may get burned if it is short securities that rise rapidly. Conversely, a fund that buys only defensive industries may not provide a full hedge to the extent you need. In my opinion, you should tread lightly and buy carefully in the world of contrarian funds. In a mutual fund portfolio, a good "all around" fund which has performed well in bulls and bears is probably preferable.

Defensive investing involves the belief that not all asset classes will do well in all markets and the knowledge that it is impossible to exactly predict which will be the next class to outperform—bonds, stocks, commodities, foreign currencies, et cetera. Therefore, we should position ourselves to perform well in a variety of market conditions. Most baseball seasons are won with lots of base hits and only the occasional exciting home run. Except for the rare superstar, those who swing for the fence at every bat seem to strike out an awful lot and frequently get really sore arms. Consistency is better than trying to make a killing in the market.

Insurance and Risk

5

When buying a home most of us call an insurance agent to protect ourselves against fire, theft, and other losses. Why? Because we can't really afford the catastrophic loss of such a large investment. We buy insurance so that we can sleep at night without worrying too much about losing something critically important to us.

We buy insurance out of fear. Is this irrational? Maybe, but it depends on your point of view. Insurance companies will not be profitable if they have too many claims. They carefully calculate the chances of your house burning down, the likelihood that you'll die before a given age, and the probability of your car being hit by another this year. Insurance is a way to calm our fears of being the one in ten million (or whatever the statistic is for the particular hazard we are worrying about) who fate selects.

In some ways the market is far more brutal than most insurable property and casualty hazards. When it strikes, it often hits everyone at once. Even worse, sometimes people who see their portfolios on fire make the situation worse by selling their holdings and fanning the fire. The flames spread through the whole neighborhood, stopping only when there are no other homes to burn, or so it seems. No insurance company in the world would be willing to insure such a risk, since every policyholder would make a claim at the same time and bankrupt the company once a decade or so. Yet the market is one of the things that we do fear the most, rational or not. How can we insure against that fear?

By definition, to insure against a loss, three basic steps must be taken:

1. Identify risk. What could cause the loss?
2. Quantify the potential loss, the value of what is at stake.
3. Act to reduce the risk of loss to within acceptable limits.

The remainder of this chapter will outline the types of risks inherent to the market. The next chapter will help you decide just what your exposure is and hopefully assist you in setting a course of action. Then, we'll spend some time on specific strategies to use.

Most people think of risk simply as the possibility that their investments will lose value. However, it is better to use a more accurate definition, with some important key words. Risk is the degree of uncertainty of the eventual return on any given investment. Note the words "uncertainty" and "eventual"—volatility and risk decrease significantly over time, both in individual investment vehicles and the broad markets, so the uncertainty of return declines over time. Successful investing demands that time and diversification be used to weather short term risks.

It is important to identify which categories and types of risk are of concern to you, because you need to hedge against that which you view as a threat, not something that is of no concern. Just as you probably shouldn't buy flood insurance if you live in the middle of the high desert, you don't need to worry about international currency risk if your entire portfolio is invested in U.S. companies who do business only within our borders. (However, you might want to think about broadening your horizons as prudent diversification.) You should also learn about types of risk you may not be aware of, to hedge against the unexpected or unknown factors that can often be more devastating than what you know.

In the financial markets, there are two broad categories of risk, systematic and unsystematic. Generally, a systematic risk affects all, or most, types of investments. Examples include interest rates, economic conditions, political events, inflation, and broad market risk. A major political event (new party gains majority in Congress, a major assassination, war, et cetera) could lower all investment prices. If the general economy is in major recession, most stocks will be depressed. It is difficult to anticipate systematic risk, since by definition it is unpredictable and pervasive in the markets. However, it is possible to hedge against systematic risk and invest defensively to outperform the broad averages when it strikes. I'll outline some strategies for this in coming chapters.

Unsystematic risk is sometimes called "specific" risk, because it affects only a single company or industry. Unsystematic risk is what most people associate with investment risk, since it is both the easiest to understand and hedge against. The first line of defense against unsystematic risk is diversification, across industries, countries, and types of security.

Here are some examples of unsystematic risk that you may want to keep in mind:

> Business risk is the possibility that a company's basic concept or operations will not generate enough sales and profits to continue growing.

Default or credit risk covers the ability of the company to cover its obligations. A highly leveraged company may pay so much to its creditors that there is not sufficient earnings to pay dividends, expand the business, et cetera.

Country risk is the possibility that a foreign government or economy may experience turmoil, hurting the companies or stock prices in that country. It is interesting to note that from our point of view, a foreign country's economic problems may be unsystematic risk, although an investor within that country would be experiencing risk systematic to her entire market. In an extreme case, country risk entails the nationalization (government takeover) of private industry.

Currency exchange rates are very real risks in today's global environment. If you own stock on the Japanese exchange that you had to buy in yen, the value of that stock could fluctuate wildly in dollar terms just due to exchange rates between the currencies even if the stock itself remained stable. Also, remember that many "domestic" American companies are now multinational players—McDonald's, Microsoft, General Electric, and most other large industrial companies have international operations which must operate with the local currency. Foreign workers and suppliers want to be paid in the local currency they can spend, and customers in those countries will obviously only buy products with their own country's money. Thus, many of our domestic companies are forced to become players in the international foreign exchange markets which, if not executed well, exposes them to currency risk.

Reinvestment risk describes the possibility that you may not be able to reinvest at similar rates when your investment comes due. For instance, let's say that you bought $10,000 of a 15 year bond in the early 1980s. The bond carried a 10% yield, meaning that you received $1,000 of income each year from your investment. However, the bond is now maturing, so you are getting your principal of $10,000 back. Interest rates have fallen, and a new 15 year bond issued by the same company now pays only 6%. You must reinvest the money to earn any income at all, but your annual income on the same investment is now only $600, which could change things dramatically if you are living on a fixed income. Reinvestment could be considered a systematic risk in that current interest rates affect a very broad range of investments. However, in looking at an individual security you must consider its maturity, dividend, payment schedule, et cetera to determine the likelihood that you will be able to reinvest its proceeds favorably in the future.

Not every type of risk applies to every security, but you should train yourself to *identify*, *quantify*, and *reduce* risk whenever you can.

Now that you know the basics of risk, let's find out what's really bothering you.

Identifying Your Style

6

Before you hedge or insure anything, you have to figure out what you are trying to protect yourself against, and to what extent. A concept that is often referred to in the financial world is the risk/reward ratio. Basically, the theory holds that as perceived risks rise, so should the potential returns over time. This is because investors will demand incrementally higher returns for increasing risks of losing their capital, or simply for experiencing volatility in their capital investment. (Incidentally, risk and its management are fascinating subjects which are worth taking the time to truly understand, since risk touches virtually every decision and action in modern life. I strongly recommend the book *Against the Gods* by Peter Bernstein for a landmark exploration of the human race's concept of and response to risk. Also, Amost Tversky and David Kahneman published excellent papers on behavioral finance.)

Let's use an insurance analogy again. If you feel that the risk of an earthquake in your area is high, you will probably want to buy earthquake insurance for your home. But if everyone else believes that the risk of earthquake is high, that insurance is going to be much more expensive than if you lived in a place that has no faults and had never had an earthquake. The greater the perceived risk, generally the more expensive the insurance. However, if your perception about the risk is correct and you have a large earthquake which demolishes your home, your "reward" (being able to afford to rebuild) will be great compared to the person who did not "invest" in the insurance.

Similarly, if you ask your insurance agent about ways to reduce the premiums you pay, one solution is to buy a policy with a higher deductible. The deductible, of course, is the portion of the loss that you have to pay before the insurance takes effect. If you have a $250 deductible, the insurance company will pay for any covered loss in excess of $250. If something happens that costs $200 to remedy, there's no use in even turning in a claim. If you have the same exact policy but carry a $1,000 deductible, the insurance company will probably charge you a smaller premium, since you are in effect saying that you are going to take care of all the "little" (less than $1,000) losses, and will only require the insurance company to step in if something really major occurs. This is often called "catastrophic" insurance, since you pay less in order to insure against the total loss of your property, but aren't insured for less significant damage.

Similar principles hold true in the marketplace. If there is a consensus that a security or the market in general is overpriced, it will cost you more to hedge against a decline than in times when everyone thinks that everything will continue to rise. This is basic supply and demand. Hedging strategies involve securities with certain attributes which may come into greater demand if everyone is trying to hedge at the same time, driving up the cost of putting the hedge in place.

Ironically, there is a widely accepted theory, often supported by history, that says that the more bearish people are, the more staying power the market has. The rationale is that when there are investors who think the market will fall, there is still money on the sidelines waiting to buy on pullbacks, providing support and maybe even further gains. Institutional money managers may begin selling if it seems that everyone believes that the market is going up forever. Their rationale is that all the money is already invested, leaving little room for future gains. Some of the widely watched indicators of investor sentiment are the ratio of puts to calls on the options exchanges and a survey which is conducted each month by a company called "Consensus, Inc.".

Hedging your investments also requires that you choose a "deductible" that you are comfortable with. You need to decide how much of a decline you can absorb. This may be more difficult than it sounds. I have heard many people say that they can tolerate 20% volatility, yet I get telephone calls from them with panicked sell orders when the market pulls back only 5 or 6%. Look deep inside, and if possible remember how you have reacted in situations which might be emotionally similar.

Decide what your risk tolerance is, and be realistic. Much of this comes from developing a fundamental investment philosophy which you really believe. Make sure that your philosophy recognizes that pullbacks are a part of normal, even healthy, market behavior. Most of my institutional clients have a very specific and detailed investment policy statement which is written and updated from time to time. I believe that it is valuable for individuals to do the same.

Besides the absolute percentage risk tolerance, you must also figure your tolerance for risk over time. Many people who claim to be able to handle a 10% pullback panic if the same percentage decline occurs too quickly. Seeing the Dow Jones Industrial Average drop 400 points (about 5% with the Dow at 8000) in one day is a lot more shocking to some people than watching it go down 40 points a day for two weeks, though the net effect is the same. Conversely, a drawn out decline which seems to be a trend is more likely to spook others, since we tend to extrapolate market direction indefinitely in both directions. When the market falls 1,000 points, is it going all the way to zero? No. Conversely, when the Dow starts rising more than 1% per day for several days in a row, does that mean that it will go on indefinitely and the Dow will be over 100,000,000 by the year 2000? (Do the math—compound returns do wonders.) Of course not—but that is how many people behave!

I could go on, but hopefully I've already convinced you to stay invested in the market. So aside from simply deciding how much absolute pain you can tolerate, you must decide how long you are willing to put up with that pain. How high is your fear quotient? Once you have a realistic sense of your risk tolerance, you will need to translate that into numbers which relate to the market in order to hedge. Let's run through a few scenarios:

You are in the market for the long term and don't normally worry about corrections much since you dollar cost average, invest on an ongoing basis, and are well diversified. However, you are afraid that if the market really pulls back this year, you might get into trouble because you have a large margin loan against your portfolio to put your daughter through her (finally!) last year of college. You need to figure out a way to protect yourself from such a short term move, which could force you to sell securities at exactly the wrong time to meet a margin call.

In a case like this, it is relatively simple to hedge, since you have an absolute percentage risk tolerance and a specific time horizon. You can simply pay an "insurance" premium by buying puts on the broad market or your individual holdings, and having them expire when you no longer feel that you need the hedge (i.e., when you are able to pay off the margin loan, your daughter has graduated, et cetera). Let's assume that the S&P 500 index is at 700 and that you have a broad portfolio which will probably move roughly with that index. Say your tolerance is for a 5% pullback. You'll want to find a way to mitigate any loss below the 665 level (700 -5%) on the S&P 500. In the next chapters, there are several ideas which can help you accomplish this—index puts, shorting S&P depository receipts, and principal protected investing.

You are worried about the market—it has doubled since just a few years ago, when you remember the Dow was around 3000. Of course, you sold everything and "got out" at 4500 when you were sure the market was in for a fall. You've been in cash ever since. You want to reinvest, but you're scared to death about getting back in. What if the crash you've been expecting for three years happens right after you invest? You feel paralyzed.

If this describes you, please close this book now. Come back when you've repented of trying to time the market. Okay, now that you've overcome this personal problem, go ahead and invest! You have to go out on a limb—that's where most of the fruit is. You might want to learn about basic defensive investing, especially types of securities which offer upside while protecting your principal on a relative basis during downturns. If you are still nervous, then average back in over time.

You have a large portfolio and are about five years from retirement. You have enough to retire comfortably on, with just a few more good years. Thus, you need to stay invested for growth to reach your goals, but can't really afford a hit to your principal this late in the game.

Though you haven't committed the sin of trying to time the market, you need to know about many of the same things as the previous example. Additionally, if you have a portfolio that has worked well to get you where you are, find out how to protect it with married puts on individual stocks or on the market as a whole. Also, variations on strategies such as shorting and covered calls might be helpful.

When you changed jobs last year you received a large rollover from your former company's 401k plan, most of which was in that company's stock. You want to hold on to it since the company has been growing consistently ahead of the market. However, the stock has historically been quite volatile and overreacted to bad news. This company probably has a long way to go before its growth slows, but you don't want to get caught should its fortunes change suddenly.

This is a case of identified unsystematic risk—you are concerned about the fortunes of one company, as opposed to the market as a whole. If you are still bullish on the overall industry the company is in, you could use a variety of strategies, such as narrow sector puts (semiconductor index, for instance) or a put on the company's stock. If your concerns center on the health of the industry as a whole, find one of the company's competitors who you think may not be doing as well and short their stock. The rationale behind these strategies are in the chapters on "Stops and Married Puts" and "Shorting."

In the past five years, you have had a pretty incredible record, with just a couple of small "blips" here and there: year one up 44%, year two down 29%, year three up 34%, year four down 18%, and year five up 20%. People always gather around you at cocktail parties to hear the latest, since you are obviously well connected. You have seven stockbrokers, because you want more than one source of new ideas to trade. For some reason all of your brokers dote on you.

How did this guy get in here? Get out of my book! Come back when you are more concerned with avoiding financial suicide than impressing your neighbors. There are several things I say to those people who tell me about their great "track records." First, absolute returns in any given year are not an indicator of long term success. As a matter of fact, it has been my experience that those who seek instant gratification often doom themselves to poor long term performance. Second, I point out the effect that aggressive short term trading can have on a portfolio:capital losses, disadvantageous tax treatment, large trading costs, and a large expenditure of time and worry. Third, I have noticed that those who are driven to tell others about their investment returns are often leaving out substantial losses that they are embarrassed about. To illustrate the power of consistency, let's look at some case studies.

A few people in most groups argue with me that the above would give an overall return of about 51% (44-29+34-18+20=51).

I dispatch those people to remedial math. The reality of a portfolio with those numbers looks like this, assuming a $10,000 starting portfolio and using a simple annual compounding:

Year	Principal balance	Gain/loss (%)	$
1	$10,000.00	44%	$4,400.00
2	14,400.00	-29%	(4,176.00)
3	10,224.00	34%	3,476.16
4	13,700.00	-18%	(2,466.03)
5	11,234.13	20%	2,246.83
		Ending balance	$13,480.96
		Average return	6.96%

Now, let's see what happens to a really "boring" portfolio that doesn't ever make big gains, but also avoids substantial loss:

Year	Principal balance	Gain/loss (%)	$
1	$10,000.00	10%	$1,000.00
2	11,000.00	9%	935.00
3	11,935.00	10%	1,193.50
4	13,128.50	7%	919.00
5	14,047.50	9%	1,264.27
	Ending balance	$15,311.77	
	Average return	10.62%	

In the above examples, you would have more money after year five had you made a compounded 8 or 9% per year in each of those years ($1.53 per $1 invested versus $1.35). Even better, I somehow suspect that you would have taken a whole lot less risk, paid much less in commissions, and had a lot more fun doing your taxes than the trader in the example. If this was in a taxable account, you should add the effect of capital gains taxes. The volatility of the portfolio in our example probably indicates a high degree of trading and hence realization of gains and losses.

The effect of taxes on a trading portfolio.

Year	Principal balance	Gain/Loss (%)	$	Taxes@28%	Net
1	$10,000.00	44%	$4,400.00	1,232.00	$3,168.00
2	$13,168.00	-29%	(3,818.72)	0.00	(3,818.72)
3	$9,349.28	34%	3,178.76	890.05	2,288.70
4	$11,637.98	-18%	(2,094.84)	0.00	(2,094.84)
5	$9,543.15	20%	1,908.63	534.42	1,374.21
		Ending Balance	$11,451.78		
		Net Average Return	2.90%		

You might argue that the above scenario is incorrect, because it leaves out the effects of carry forward loss provisions in our nation's ever changing tax code. To a limited extent, you are allowed to carry forward prior year's losses against current capital gains. This does make a bit of difference to the results, but unfortunately, not much. When losses are carried forward in this case and applied against the taxes in future years, it does improve that net average annual return to a whopping 4.66%, or about $1.23 versus every dollar invested five years earlier.

The effect of taxes on a trading portfolio, using loss carry forward provision.

Year	Principal balance	Gain/Loss (%)	$	Taxes@28%	Net
1	$10,000.00	44%	$4,400.00	1,232.00	$3,168.00
2	$13,168.00	-29%	(3,818.72)	0.00	(3,818.72)
3	$9,349.28	34%	3,178.76	0.00	3,178.76
4	$12,528.07	-18%	(2,255.05)	0.00	(2,255.05)
5	$10,272.99	20%	2,054.60	0.00	2,054.60
		Ending Balance	$12,327.59		
		Net Average Return	4.66%		

This is still less than half the return of our long term investor who was making "only" 8 to 10% per year but recognizing no short term gains.

As I write this, some money market funds are yielding around 5.4%, or about 4% net after income taxes. Several high quality tax-free money market funds are yielding well above 3.3%. In any taxable account, this should provide a pretty clear perspective on the downfalls of heavy trading, unless the gains are consistent and substantial every single year.

Also, the amount of losses you can carry forward each year are limited to $3,000. If you are dealing with a portfolio of any size the net effect of taxes is more pronounced even if losses are carried forward. Using the same rates of return as in the prior examples, we see that short term taxes take ever larger bites of large portfolios.

The effect of taxes on a trading portfolio.

Year	Principal balance	Gain/Loss (%)	$	Taxes@28%	Net
1	$100,000.00	44%	$44,000.00	12,320.00	$31,680.00
2	$13,1680.00	-29%	(38,187.20)	0.00	(38,187.20)
3	$93,492.80	34%	31,787.55	5,900.51	25,887.04
4	$119,379.84	-18%	(21,488.37)	0.00	(21,488.37)
5	$97,891.47	20%	19,578.29	2,481.92	17,096.37
		Ending Balance	$117,469.76		
		Net Average Return	3.49%		

Using a starting balance of $100,000 and generating the same returns in prior examples will leave us with a net average annual return of only 3.49%, or about $1.17 for each dollar invested five years ago. Short term gains rates move higher for individuals with high income or larger amounts of gains. The money market funds are looking quite good about now!

Short term trading in tax deferred portfolios like IRAs and other retirement accounts doesn't have the tax implications, but the risks to capital are the same. While I do engage in short term trading, it is only as a part of a larger portfolio strategy. Without core long term holdings to build upon, I believe that most portfolios which are heavily traded are doomed to substantial underperformance or even outright failure.

For the trader in this example, all I can say is that I hope he had fun while he was trading. For those of you who enjoy this type of fun, might I suggest a gambling establishment? Sometimes they even serve free drinks and hor d'ouevres while you play!

Being an intelligent investor, you notice that the return on the S&P 500 has been about 14.8% per year including dividends for the past decade. If you could duplicate that type of return, you would be quite happy. You're aware that the S&P's total return has included some dips, but you're in this for the long term anyway.

In the chapter entitled "Bored MBSs" there are descriptions of several securities and strategies which do track the S&P 500, and they are often more liquid than index funds. They can be very useful when used as the "base" component for an overall portfolio of more actively managed stocks. A word of caution is in order, however. In my opinion, the recent popularity of so-called "index" funds may be dangerous for the very indexes they track. Investment managers must buy the stocks which make up a given index in order to match the performance of that index. (The S&P 500 is the index which most managers are using as their benchmark, though the Russell 2000 and other broader indices are used by some.) Certain indices may become overvalued compared to stocks which are not members of the index but have similar businesses, growth rates, et cetera. This can make the underlying index, and hence the stocks within it, much more volatile than it should be, and exaggerates moves both to the upside and the downside.

You have the portfolio that most investors dream of, with fifteen core blue chip stocks which you have held for an average of a decade each. Needless to say, you are incredibly profitable on them, especially since you have employed dividend reinvestment and have built up some very impressive positions. You want to gradually shift a substantial portion of your assets into a laddered municipal bond portfolio to provide for a very comfortable retirement income. You don't want to take the capital gains on your stocks all at once, but want to be assured that your portfolio is worth at least as much in the future as it is today.

Several strategies apply to you—especially collars, covered calls, and variations on shorting. If your portfolio is of substantial value (one million or more), retain the services of one of the major investment banks. Though it might seem initially expensive, they can offer a variety of other solutions in the form of exchange funds, securities lending, forward hedging, and the like, that are not available to the average investor.

• • • • • • •

There are as many scenarios as individual investors, so this chapter could go on for volumes. The key is to identify what kind of investor you are. If you have some habits or beliefs that are hindering your long term performance, change them. Then, get educated and use common sense strategies to maximize your return by minimizing your risk. The remaining chapters of this book will hopefully help you to learn some of these strategies in detail!

Stops and Married Puts

7

Because of my broad experience in asset allocation, trading, and years of research and back testing, I can say for a surety that every stock will always do one of five things, although to varying degrees and for different time periods. Ready? Here it is: *a stock will go up a lot, up a little, down a lot, down a little, or do nothing*. Now you know.

Why do I make such an inane observation? Well, because an even simpler observation follows. If you could only remove your exposure to the case in which a stock goes down a lot, then what would be left? The ones that go up a little and the ones that go down a little will pretty much cancel each other out. So you have the ones that don't do much (well, let's hope they pay a dividend) and the ones that go up a lot. Basically, your portfolio has a net profit. So, how do you hedge? We'll examine many strategies, both time honored and recently developed.

Stopping losses before they start

One classic trading strategy involves placing what is called a "stop" order with your broker. A stop becomes an active sell order (It is possible to use stops and limits on buy orders, though I will not discuss them in that context here.) when its price is reached or passed. For instance, if a stock you own is trading at

$55, and you have a stop order to sell it at $50, nothing will happen unless the stock trades down to or below $50. When the stock touches $50, your order becomes an active sell order. Since the order becomes a market order, your trade could actually occur above or below your stop price. If the stock is moving quickly, it is entirely possible that a $50 stop order could cause an execution of $49.75 or even $50.25.

To control the price at which your trade may be executed if the stop becomes an active order, you can add a "limit" qualifier. The limit tells the broker that you are willing to sell at a certain price (or better) if the stop price is touched. So, a $50 Stop, $50 Limit order would instruct the broker to sell your stock at $50 or more if (and only if) the stock trades at $50 or less.

But what if your stock closes at $52, but opens the next day much lower than your stop at $50? Let's assume that the stock begins trading again at $45. If you have a stop order only, you will sell at the market and probably get around $45 a share, since the price has passed the "trigger" of $50 which activates your sell order. If you have a $50 Stop, $50 Limit order, your sell order will become active but it will be an order to sell only if the stock can be sold at $50 or more again. To summarize stop and stop limit orders, here are some examples:

Stop order	Limit order	Stock price	Result
STOP 50	none	$55	no trade - stock is above trigger price
STOP 50	LIMIT 50	55	no trade - stock is above trigger price
STOP 50	none	50	stock will be sold at the market price
STOP 50	LIMIT 50	50	stock will probably be sold at $50
STOP 50	none	45	stock will be sold at the market price
STOP 50	LIMIT 50	45	order to sell at $50 or more will become active

Stop and stop limit orders, like most other buy and sell orders, can be placed with a broker on a "day" or "good till cancelled" basis. A day order is valid only for the trading day during which it is placed, and must be renewed each day in order to stay in effect. A "good till canceled" (referred to as "GTC") order remains active until you notify your broker that you no longer want it to be in effect. I recommend a review of all such orders on regular basis.

Marrying your stock

Another popular hedging strategy uses a "married" put option. The options are contracts which are based on a stock that you own. Since you buy the option specifically to hedge a given part of your portfolio, it is referred to as a "married" position.

If you buy a put option you have purchased the right to sell your stock to someone else at a predetermined price through a specified date. For instance, if you buy a "March 30" put option you have the right to sell your stock (or "put" it to someone else) at $30 per share through a certain day in March.

If you are not familiar with options in general, here's a quick primer:

Each option is referred to as a contract, since you are paying someone in exchange for them agreeing to do something (i.e., buy or sell stock) at a set price in the future. Options contracts are available in five point increments—i.e., there are strike prices at 20, 25, 30, 35, 40, et cetera.

For lower priced stocks the options come in 2 1/2 point increments, and occasionally you will see other strike prices which result when there is a split in the stock or other special circumstance.

There are two types of options—puts and calls. It is important to understand the basic definition of each. We'll discuss calls later, but for now remember that a put gives you the right, but not the obligation, to "put" (sell) your stock to someone at the specified price should you choose to do so, regardless of where the stock is currently trading.

Every option contract represents 100 shares of the underlying stock, so if you want to buy a put to protect 500 shares of ABC Company you will want to buy five contracts.

Shares of Stock	Option Contracts
100	1
200	2
500	5
1,000	10

Also, options are quoted "per share," but since each one actually represents 100 shares you must multiply the option price you see by 100. For instance, if an option is quoted at $3^1/_2$, the money needed to purchase that option is actually $350 ($3.50 x 100 shares).

Option Quote Price (Decimal)	Option Quote Price (Fraction)	Cost to Purchase ($)
1	1	$ 100
5	5	500
10	10	1,000
0.125	$^1/_8$	12.5
.25	$^1/_4$	25
.375	$^3/_8$	37.5
.75	$^3/_4$	75
.9375	$^{15}/_{16}$	93.75

All stock options stop trading on the third Friday of the month in which they expire; the following Monday they are worth nothing, because the contract has expired.

Options on the U.S. exchanges are liquid, meaning you can generally sell them anytime up to the close of trading on their expiration date (This is called an American style option, as opposed to a European option which is settled only at its expiration date). They will normally move up and down in price in parity with the stock. Also, the prices of most option contracts are quoted on an exchange, so like stock transactions we don't know who is the counterparty to our buy or sell.

Options symbols are quoted differently than stock. If you are using an online service or other medium in which you must have the symbol to get a quote, be aware that options are quoted with five position tickers, of which the first three positions tell you which stock the option represents, the fourth tells you which month the option expires, and the fifth is the strike price. For instance, "DISAL" is the symbol for Disney (DIS) January (A) $60 strike (L) (The symbols for all the months and strikes for both calls and puts are listed in the appendix). Knowing two other things will help you avoid confusion.

First, for stocks which have only one or two letters in their ticker symbol (C for Chrysler, GE for General Electric, et cetera) only that ticker is used, so for Chrysler options the option symbol would have only three positions (C, plus the month, plus the strike) and GE would have four (GEAL=General Electric January 60 call). Second, since there are only three positions for the stock in the option symbol, NASDAQ listed companies, which have four letters in their stock symbol, have been assigned different symbols for their options. For instance, Microsoft (MSFT) is "MSQ," and Intel (INTC) is "INQ." Ask your broker or use a search function to find the proper symbol to use, but do make sure that you are using the correct one. Appendices A and B contain some of these. (I suggest obtaining a copy of a brochure entitled "Characteristics and Risks of Standardized Options" which is published by the Chicago Board Options Exchange (CBOE). Copies are available through most brokerages, by calling (800) 678-4667, or writing to: Chicago Board Options Exchange, 400 South LaSalle Street, Chicago, IL 60605.)

It is important to have a basic understanding of the above information before moving on. If you do, then let's walk through an example of hedging your stock position with a married put.

You bought 250 shares of a great company called Yowza Software (ticker symbol YWZ) several years ago, and since you chose a dividend reinvestment program you now have exactly 300 shares with a cost basis of about $12 overall. The stock is trading at $43, and although you think that the company is doing better than ever, you want to protect your profit to at least $40 until June "just in case." To hedge this position until the June expiration, you will need to buy three puts since you own 300 shares) at a strike price of $40, the lowest you are willing to sell the stock. Let's say that you find out that the June 40 puts are trading at $2, or $200 ($2 x 100 shares) apiece. So, to hedge your position you would purchase three YWZ June 40 puts ("YWZRH" for those of you who checked the table).

Now, let's figure out some scenarios. Best case, the stock continues to rise between now and the expiration, and when the option expires it's trading at $65! Well, I guess you wasted money on the put option, kind of like paying an insurance premium but never having to file a claim on the policy. But was it really wasted? You had peace of mind that your financial position in that stock was protected, at least until June.

Worst case, you will be able to sell your stock at an effective price of $38 by "putting" your stock using your option contract any time before June. Why $38 and not $40? Since you spent $2 per share to buy the option, your net realized price is the strike price ($40) less the cost of the option ($2). If the stock dropped to $30 and you didn't think it was going to come back, you would do this.

Stock position
Own 300 shares of YWZ at average cost of $12
The stock has risen to more than $40 per share.

Married put option to hedge stock position
Bought three put contracts for YWZ, expiring in June with a strike price of $40.

Stock drops to $30
Exercise puts, which give you the right

	Quantity	Price	Value
Unhedged	300	$30	$9,000
Hedged with Put	300	$40	$12,000

Basically, a put contract purchased on stock which you own creates a "floor" price, below which you are not exposed to the market fluctuations of the stock. Thus, your realized value per share of stock will not fall below the strike price of the put contract minus what you had to pay for the contract:

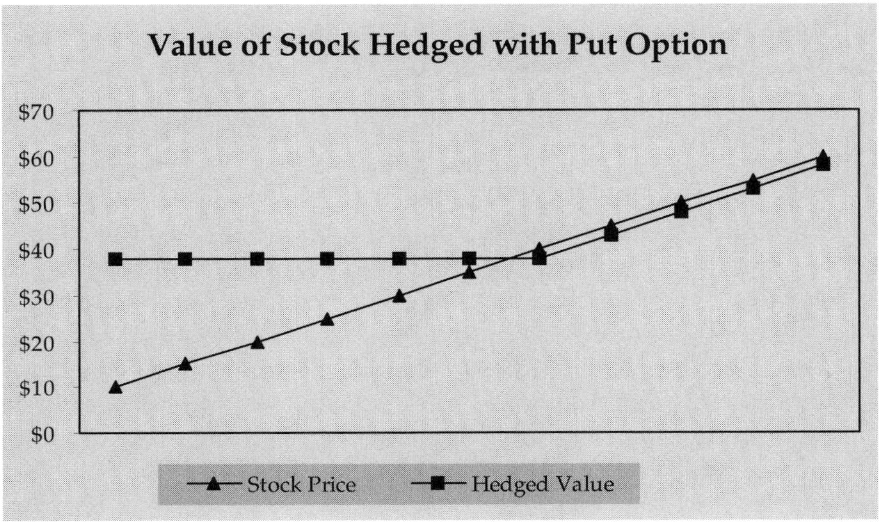

Yet there is an alternative to actually selling your stock and realizing a capital gain on the entire position. If you think that the decline in the stock is only short term and want to remain an investor in the company, you could simply sell your put option. If the stock is trading at $30 and the option allows you to sell the same stock at $40, then you know that this option will have a value of at least $10 per share, since anyone buying it from you could simply buy the stock at the market price ($30) and use the option to sell it at the strike price ($40), instantly realizing a $10 gain. We call this the "intrinsic" value of the option.

In reality, of course, the option will usually trade at a slight premium to its intrinsic value, since there is a value in the "time" aspect of an option contract. Remember, we paid $2 for an option that gave us the right to sell at $40 when the stock was trading at $43 in the open market. Our option had no intrinsic value, but we were willing to pay for it to hedge ourselves, while other people who didn't own the stock would pay for the option just to speculate that the stock was going to fall.

So, if the stock fell to $30 before June we could probably sell it for its intrinsic value ($10) plus whatever "time" premium the market had placed on the option. If everyone seemed to think that the stock was going down even further, then speculators would probably drive the price of this option up, since it would be worth more the further the stock fell.

So, if your stock goes up, congratulations! You made a lot of money and slept better at night because you were hedged. However, if it goes down a lot, you have some choices to make. You can either "put" the stock using your option (this is called "exercising" your option, or exercising your right to sell the stock at the strike price), or you can simply sell the option at its market price (thus transferring your right to sell to someone else) and keep the profit on the option while retaining ownership of your shares and avoiding the tax consequences on the sale of your very appreciated stock position. Let's look at an example of the former.

Sell stock at market or exercise option, whichever will return more. Assuming option cost $2 per contract and $12 cost basis on stock. Strike price on put option is $40.

Current Stock Price	**Put (sell) stock?**	**Stock sold (net per sh)**	**Realized (taxable gain)**
20	Yes	$38	$ 7,200
30	Yes	38	7,200
35	Yes	38	7,200
40	No	40	7,800
50	No	50	10,800
60	No	60	13,800

Again, if you are convinced that the decline in the stock is temporary and you would like to remain a shareholder, you are better off simply selling the option and keeping your stock. You will have made a profit on the option that will offset the decline in the stock, and if the decline is indeed temporary you will have, in effect, profited on the way down and on the way up!

One other benefit is that you will have sold only the option, which means that you will not have to realize the gain on your stock for tax purposes. Of course, if you have owned the option for less than a year you will pay short term capital gains tax on it, but if you have a very low cost basis in the stock that is still preferable to realizing the larger capital gain in the stock. What you don't owe won't hurt you.

Sell put (3 contracts at $40 strike price) and retain stock (300 shares), assuming option cost $2 per contract and $12 cost basis on stock.

Current stock price	Stock Value (unrealized)	Current Value (opt + stock)	Realized (taxable gain)
$20	$ 6,000	$12,000	$5,400
30	9,000	12,000	2,400
35	10,500	12,000	900
40	12,000	12,000	0
50	15,000	15,000	0
60	18,000	18,000	0
70	21,000	21,000	0

Some examples of when buying a married put might be appropriate:

A hot young growth company is going to release its quarterly earnings next month; analysts have very high expectations, and historically the stock has lost 30% or more of its value when it disappoints the analysts. A married put will protect you if the stock falls, but allow you all the upside if the company beats expectations and resumes its meteoric rise. Keep in mind that on more volatile stocks, other investors and speculators will be buying the options as well, making them more expensive.

It's December, and you want to sell your position in XYZ because you think the company's management is failing. You have a substantial gain in the stock since you bought it in August, but your CPA tells you that any more short term capital gains will have horrible tax consequences. The option can essentially "lock" the price of the stock for you; if it falls, you call sell it for your option strike price when you exercise it in the future, delaying the realization of your gain until the next tax year. If your stock rises, congratulations on selling it for a long term capital gain at a higher price than you could have today.

Buying married puts isn't the only answer. In fact, it can be quite expensive. Marrying a put to everything in your portfolio is like buying too much insurance on everything in your home, even things that are at very low risk of being lost. If you "overinsure," you eventually end up paying for what you are trying to insure all over again. Buy puts only on positions which you believe are at a real risk of temporary loss. If you believe that a failure at the company could cause the stock to be permanently or irretrievably hurt, reevaluate your tolerance for the risk position in the stock and consider if you should actually be selling the position now instead of hedging it with options or other strategies.

Index puts

Now you know how to hedge against a decline in an individual stock by purchasing a put "married" to a specific stock position. But what if your real concern is about the entire market? As you may guess, put options also exist on more than just individual stocks.

An index is not a tradeable security by itself, but is how the performance of certain industries or sectors can be tracked. However, there are often other securities, such as options, futures, and other derivatives, which are based on a certain index and are traded in the markets.

Indices are basically averages based on the prices of a selected group of stocks which fit the individual parameters of the index. Your portfolio probably won't ever contain all the stocks in any one index, but finding an index which "looks" like your portfolio can be a valuable way to both track and hedge your portfolio. For instance, the XCI (AMEX Computer Technology) index is "a narrow based capitalization-weighted index of the top 26 producers of computers and computer related equipment." (Courtesy American Exchange.) It contains such companies as Microsoft, Intel, Apple, Micron, Oracle, Hewlett Packard, and IBM.

If you own technology stocks, you may notice that over time the general direction of your stocks and this index seem to be parallel. The degree of the similarity is often referred to as the "correlation" of the index to your portfolio. If the correlation is low and your stocks are not keeping up with the index, you may want to make some changes so that you own the leaders in the group, not the laggards. A low correlation could also indicate that the index simply does not have much in common with your portfolio.

Let's assume that you do own quite a few mid to large capitalization technology stocks, most of which fit the description of the XCI index. To provide at least a partial hedge for those holdings, you could buy insurance on your portfolio by purchasing a put option on the index. If the index is truly correlated to your portfolio, this should provide a fairly strong hedge against major declines. Let's use the XCI index to walk through an example. Incidentally, the XCI was established with a base value of 100 on July 29, 1983, and is now above 400. Great returns, though the ride in technology stocks has been a bit bumpier than the norm.

To buy a put on the XCI may be comparably expensive since it has been quite volatile on its way up. High levels of volatility in the underlying security or index makes options have larger time premiums, since people are betting on probable outcomes when buying options. A very volatile stock or index has a larger possibility of reaching a price objective than a more stable or slow moving one.

For instance, if index ABC has traded from 100 to 150, back to 110, then back to 150 in the past year, people may be willing to pay quite a lot for a 130 put, since it seems possible that the index may fall past that point and make the owner of that option a lot of money. On the other hand, if index XYZ has traded in a narrow range of 145 to 155 for the last three years, the 130 puts on XYZ might be comparably inexpensive because it seems less feasible that the index will reach that price before expiration.

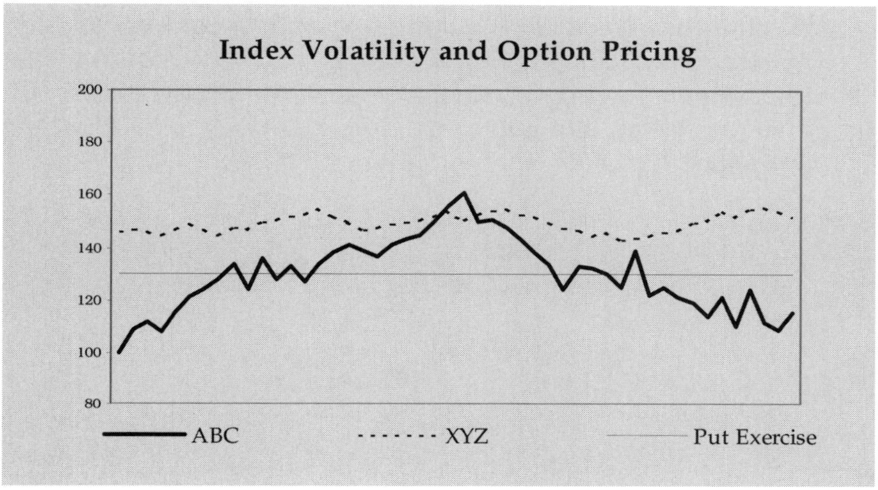

It is obvious to see that ABC is more volatile than XYZ, so a put option on ABC will be more expensive. The likelihood of a stock or index reaching a certain price given its history is going to contribute to the price of the option. If it seems likely to reach the option "strike" or exercise price (like ABC) it will be more expensive than if the underlying stock or index seems very unlikely to reach that price (like XYZ).

Back to the XCI. Let's say that it is March and you want to hedge your technology stocks through December against anything greater than a 20% decline in the technology sector. If the XCI index stands at 400, you calculate that a 20% decline would put that index at 320. A put with a strike price of 320 will protect you by rising in price as the index falls and goes below that level. Why will the put be rising as the index approaches the 320 mark, and not just if it goes below it? Because the closer the index is to the strike price the more likely the outcome of the index surpassing that price, and the more people will be willing to pay to speculate on that outcome.

Before we move to an example, let's make sure that you understand exactly what we're trying to accomplish. If the technology index is falling, then logically your technology stocks are falling as well. We are hoping that the profit on the put (created by the falling index) will roughly offset the loss on your stocks, thus allowing you to keep your portfolio intact and hope for better days. Let's assume that you own the following portfolio:

Stock	Shares	Price	Net
Microsoft	100	$105	$10,500
Intel	100	150	15,000
Novell	1,200	9	10,800
Motorola	150	65	9,750
LSI Logic	400	32	12,800
Silicon Graphics	850	17	14,450
Cisco Systems	300	59	17,700
Integrated Devices	900	10	9,000
		TOTAL:	**$100,000**

Let's also say you want to hedge your positions against a 10% decline. You have decided that the XCI index has the highest correlation to your portfolio, and the XCI is currently at 400. When you look up the 360 (index at 400 less 10% = 360) puts, you get a quote of $14. Though there is no underlying stock or shares, index options are quoted in the same way as stock options, so $14 means a $1,400 outlay to buy that option.

However, how many contracts should you buy to hedge the $100,000 portfolio? Get your financial professional's input on this, but remember that each point in the index equals $100 and you can calculate the numbers easily enough. If each stock in your $100,000 portfolio drops 10%, you are down by $10,000. So, you need to buy options which should theoretically be worth roughly $10,000 if the index drops by the same amount.

To determine how many contracts are appropriate for your hedge, calculate the value of a 1% drop in both the index and your portfolio in dollar terms. A 1% drop in the XCI index (400 x .01) is 4 points, or $400.

Assumptions:

- $100,000 portfolio, primarily in tech stocks.
- High correlation (similar historical performance and holdings) to the XCI index.

	Beginning Value	Value with Decline of: 1%	5%	10%
Portfolio:	$100,000	$99,000	$95,000	$90,000
	Net Loss:	($1,000)	($5,000)	($10,000)
XCI Index:	400	396	380	360
	Gain per Contract:	$400	$2,000	$4,000
Ratio of loss in portfolio to gain per option contract		**2.5**	**2.5**	**2.5**

The same percentage represents $1,000 in your portfolio, so you will need exactly 2.5 contracts ($1,000 divided by $400) to hedge your portfolio, right? No. You have to buy at least three, since you can't trade partial options contracts. (You may even want to buy four to account for the deteriorating time value of your option—more on this later.)

Remember that in reality this option will rise in price even before the index crosses the 360 mark. However, since it may not rise on a one to one basis on the index, since its value is not intrinsic (the difference between the strike price and the current index price) until it surpasses the strike price. Assuming it is not too close to expiration, you could have a profit in the trading price of the option even if the index only drops 5%. However, for this decision you really need only think about what happens if the index goes below the level of the put contract's exercise or "strike" price. You are trying to protect yourself against catastrophic losses in excess of 10%, since you consider 10% the "deductible" that you can absorb before things begin to hurt.

Remember that your portfolio won't have exact correlation to the index unless you own every stock that is in the index, so even if the index drops a given percentage your portfolio may have dropped more or less than that amount. Let's look at an example of your portfolio with the put, assuming that you bought three XCI 360 puts at $14, the index has dropped about 20%, and the various stocks in your portfolio have lost between 15% and 40% of their value:

Stock	Shares	Price	Net
Microsoft	100	$85.0	$8,500
Intel	100	128.0	12,800
Novell	1,200	7.0	8,400
Motorola	150	48.0	7,200
LSI Logic	400	25.0	10,000
Silicon Graphics	850	12.0	10,200
Cisco Systems	300	49.0	14,700
Integrated Devices	900	9.0	8,550
		TOTAL:	$80,350

Put contract	Qty	Intrinsic value	
XCI December 36	3	4,000	$12,000

(index = 320, or a 20% decline from 40)

NET PORTFOLIO VALUE: $92,350

Perhaps you are wondering why this supposedly good hedge didn't help to keep the $7,650 between your original $100,000 and the $92,350 shown. The answer is very simple—you weren't trying to. You were only trying to protect yourself from a decline of more than 10%, which was the deductible you had decided on for this portfolio insurance. However, it is actually better than it looks.

In the real market, options prices are not based on just their intrinsic value. Remember, intrinsic value is the difference between the current price of the stock or index and the exercise price of the option. In this example, you paid $14 for the option to begin with, even though the index was 40 points away from the strike price of that option: that's the time, or speculative, value of the option, and it is not going to be completely gone unless the option is very close to expiration.

For simplicity's sake, let's assume that the time value of the option deteriorates predictably between purchase and expiration. In reality, and option's time value generally goes down faster in the last month of it's life, since the option holders can hear the clock ticking and are willing to take a lower price for their contracts.

If we bought this put for $14 when it had six months until expiration, and the index falls 20% three months into the put's life, let's say it is worth one half its original time value of $14 in addition to its intrinsic value:

Stock	Shares	Price	Net
Microsoft	100	$85.0	$8,500
Intel	100	128.0	12,800
Novell	1,200	7.0	8,400
Motorola	150	48.0	7,200
LSI Logic	400	25.0	10,000
Silicon Graphics	850	12.0	10,200
Cisco Systems	300	49.0	14,700
Integrated Devices	900	9.5	8,550
		TOTAL:	$80,350

Put contract	Qty	Intrinsic value	
XCI December 360	3	4,000	$12,000
		Time/speculative value	
	3	700	$2,100
		TOTAL OPTIONS VALUE:	$14,100
		NET PORTFOLIO VALUE:	**$92,350**

Not bad, especially if you consider that most of these companies are not going out of business and that eventually they will probably regain their losses and rise even higher. You made money on the way down and on the way up.

One note about index options, since there is no single underlying stock they settle in cash for their intrinsic value at expiration. In the example above, if the index is anywhere above 360 at expiration, the option expires worthless, but you would get $100 per contract for each point that the index is below the strike price. To be more accurate, most American style options settle in increments of $^{1}/_{16}$ of a point, or $6.25 per option. If your index is $1^{3}/_{16}$ below your strike, you get $118.75, et cetera).

Index option values (intrinsic only) at settlement/expiration on a put with a 360 strike price.

Index Quote	Value per Put Option Contract (Fractions)	(Decimal)	(Dollars)
400.000	0	0.000	$0.00
360.000	0	0.000	$0.00
359.063	15/16	0.938	$93.75
359.250	3/4	0.750	$75.00
359.375	5/8	0.625	$62.50
359.500	1/2	0.500	$50.00
359.625	3/8	0.375	$37.50
359.750	1/4	0.250	$25.00
359.875	1/8	0.125	$12.50
355.000	5	5.000	$500.00
340.000	20	20.00	$2,000.00
320.000	40	40.00	$4,000.00

The above chart shows only the intrinsic value of the option on the day it expires. A contract with many months until expiration may still retain some time or speculative value as well.

You can sell the option any time before expiration for whatever it is trading for at that time.

Covered Calls and Collars

8

A call option is the exact opposite of a put option. A call gives its owner the right, but not the obligation, to buy a stock at a given price until a specified date. Thus, a General Electric January 110 call option gives its owner the right to buy 100 shares (remember that each option contract represents 100 shares) of General Electric at $110 per share through the expiration date in January.

But how does the right to buy more stock help to hedge a position? We'll discuss some more strategies using long term calls to reduce risk in the next chapter, but for now we're not going to own the right to buy more stock. We're going to sell that right to someone else.

This can effectively "sell" our stock at a certain price, yet leave our alternatives open as to the timing (for tax purposes) or the decision to actually sell. Like most strategies, however, covered calls contain their own risks. It is important to understand the opportunity cost of writing covered calls. However, first some background.

To help you hedge an existing position, a call option can be sold. Selling a call obligates you to deliver stock at a certain price through a certain date to the owner of the call option. It is the other side of the contract described in the previous paragraphs. Selling calls for which you do not have stock to deliver is considered very risky (this is termed selling "naked" calls) and in my opinion, should be done only by people who either can afford to use $100 bills as wallpaper, who have had a lobotomy, or who are professional traders. However, selling calls "covered" by a stock position you own can be a wise choice in some cases.

Remember how you had to pay a premium over the intrinsic value of the put options in the last section? Call options are no different.

Say it is now March and you buy a call on Occidental Widgets (ticker OW) that expires in August and has a strike (exercise) price of $50. Occidental Widgets is trading at $45 when you buy the call, so it has no real intrinsic value—at that time you can buy the stock cheaper in the open market ($45) than what your option gives you ($50). Since a call offers a "free look" at the price of the stock without having to actually own shares in the company, the option will carry a premium, depending on how excited other traders are about Occidental Widgets' prospects.

Let's say the option costs $2. Why would anyone pay that when it has no intrinsic value? Well, look at the possibilities. Assume that the company makes a widget that does every unpleasant task in your life for you, and it even operates on cold fusion. Occidental Widget stock rises to $60 by August, so it has risen 33% for an investor who bought the stock back at $45. But look at the option trader—she bought an option at $2 when the stock was at $45, but at expiration the call option has an intrinsic value of $10 ($60 minus the $50 exercise price). This is a 400% return on her investment.

Comparable returns on stock versus call option

Assuming 100 shares of stock purchased at $45 (cost $4,500) and one August 50 call option purchased at $2 (cost $200)

Stock Price Expiration	Value of Stock Position ($)	Percentage Return	Value of Option Position ($)	Percentage Return	
$30	$3,000	-33%	0	-100%	(Total
35	3,500	-22%	0	-100%	Loss
40	4,000	-11%	0	-100%	of
45	4,500	0%	0	-100%	Principal
50	5,000	11%	0	-100%	Invested)
55	5,500	22%	500	150%	
60	6,000	33%	1,000	400%	
65	6,500	44%	1,500	650%	
70	7,000	56%	2,000	900%	

Of course, the risk/return ratio holds true here. Had the stock stayed below $50, the call option would be worth nothing whatsoever at expiration since all of the "time" premium would have passed. Statistically, a majority of amateur options traders lose money because, although you make a lot of money if you are right, you frequently lose the entire investment if you are wrong. This is true even if you are only wrong about the price or the timing. I've seen many cases when an option expires on a Friday, and the company stock suddenly surges the next week. This causes intense emotional pain for the option holder who lost money because even though he was right about the stock, he just didn't pay for enough time on the option.

Options trading like what I just described is generally considered very speculative and poses substantial risk of loss to your principal. To put things in perspective, if you own a call option you have a one-in-three possibility of an outcome which will create an intrinsic profit. If the underlying stock rises, you win. If it falls or stays the same, you lose. So only one in three possible scenarios yields a net profit on the intrinsic value of the option. But now let's describe how you can let other people speculate their hearts out, and pay you for the privilege.

Let's use Occidental Widget again. You bought 500 shares of the stock at $30 several years ago, and after many ups and downs you are relieved to see that it is finally at $45 per share. You would be perfectly willing to sell it, except you've heard rumors that they have a new widget coming out. Since the stock often moves up on new widget introductions, you figure that the stock might have more upside. But you are still worried that it's going to fall back to the $35 range, which it has done so many times before.

Remember the trader who is willing to pay $2 for the August 50 call, even though the stock is only trading at $45? Well, it's time to take advantage of this. You call your broker, who tells you that the Occidental Widget August 50 call options are trading for $2 each. Since you have 500 shares, you can "write" (sell) five option contracts and have shares to deliver even if the option is exercised and you have to sell them your stock. The calls you sell are covered by the 500 shares. Since each contract represents 100 shares, you are going to receive $1,000 for the sale (five contracts x 100 shares x $2 each). Now let's look at what can happen after you do this trade.

Covered call hedge

Stock position of 500 shares OW, currently trading at $545.
Sell August 50 call on OW, currently trading at $2 ($200) per contract.

Security	**Quantity**		**Price**	**Net Value**
OW	500	Shares	$45	$22,500
OW August 50 calls	5	Contracts	2	1,000
			Total:	$23,500

If the stock falls back to $35, it is obvious that no rational person is going to exercise an option to buy the stock at $50, since they can simply buy the stock at $35 in the open market. So, you will get to keep the option trader's $2 premium as profit. If you think that this fall is very temporary, you can buy the call back. If the stock has dropped from $45 to $35, the call will probably only be worth a fraction of $2, since $50 looks like a pretty high target from $35. You could then try to rebuy it, and try to sell another option contract if and when it rises again.

Covered call hedge - stock declines after call is written

When OW stock was at $45, sold 5 August 50 call options versus a long position of 500 shares OW stock; received $1,000 proceeds from sale. Call option is now trading for less due to price decline in stock.

Action	Security	Quantity		Price	Net Value
Sold	OW August	5	Contracts	$2	$1,000
Buy Back	Ow August	5	Contracts	0.25	(125)
				Total:	$875

Now, although your stock is worth substantially less (since it is trading at $35 instead of $45), you have realized a gain of $875 due to its decline and still have the stock to hold in hopes of future price appreciation. Of course, in the case of such price declines you can simply do nothing and the option will expire worthless as long as the stock remains below the $50 strike price at expiration. This is usually the safest bet. However, remember that if your stock returns to higher levels and you have repurchased the call option previously sold, you may be able to sell another call for an attractive premium at that time.

Of course, you should never sell a call at a strike price that you are not actually willing to sell your stock for at that time. If the stock rises above the strike price, the call option may be exercised, causing you to be obligated to sell your stock at $50 per share on or before the expiration date. You still get to keep your premium of $2, of course, for a total price of $52 if you want to look at it that way. If this occurs, it is referred to as being called out or called away.

In practice there are several strategies by which you can avoid getting called out of a stock, even if it has risen so much that the option is "in the money," meaning that its strike price is below the current stock price. For instance, if Occidental Widget is trading at $55 per share, you could be called out of the stock since you sold the right to buy it from you at $50. In reality, comparably few options are exercised prior to their expiration, even when they are in the money. However, you should be aware that it can happen. If someone decides to exercise an option to purchase stock prior to expiration of the option, a lottery system determines who must sell their stock to the exerciser. If you are one of the people who sold that option, there is a chance that your stock will be sold to meet that exercise notice.

I have seen in the money covered call options remain in accounts for months and years without being called away, since most traders purchase options to trade them, not to actually exercise them and buy stock. If they'd wanted the actual stock, they would have simply purchased shares in the first place. Remember, however, that on the date of expiration, *all* options that are in the money are automatically exercised. There is no chance that your option will not be exercised, so you must take action prior to the end of trading on expiration day if the stock is above the strike price and you would prefer not to sell your stock.

What do you do if you decide that you really don't want to be called out? You could buy the call back, but if the stock is at $55, the $50 call option is going to be worth at least $5 and you would take a $3 loss between the $5 cost to buy it back and the $2 you sold it for. Not very palatable, right?

But wait—maybe there's a way out. Let's return to the example above. If it is a few days before expiration in August, almost all of the time value of the call option will be gone, and the option will be trading at intrinsic value only. The call options which expire in December, however, may still have some "time" value. The December 50 calls, for instance, may be worth $7 ($5 intrinsic plus perhaps $2 time value). Maybe the December 55 calls are worth $3.50, since the stock is now at $55 and the company seems to be on a growth spurt with their new widget. Assuming these prices, we have the following scenarios on your 500 shares and the five call options:

Scenario 1—Allow your stock to be called out at $50.

Action	Security	Shares	Options	Price	Net
Sold	August 50		5	$ 2	$ 1,000
Sell	OW Stock	500		50	25,000
			TOTAL PROCEEDS:		**$26,000**

In this case, you have done nothing to prevent your stock from being "called away," and so your broker automatically sells the stock for you at the $50 strike price. You realized an effective price of $52 per share before commissions. However, if you feel that given the new direction of the company you don't want to sell right now, there are other alternatives.

Scenario 2—Buy back August 50 call, sell December 50 call.

Action	Security	Shares	Options	Price	Net
Sold	August 50		5	$2	$ 1,000
Buy	August 50		-5	5	(2,500)
Sell	December 50	5	7		3,500
			TOTAL PROCEEDS:		**$2,000**

Scenario 2 accomplishes several things, but primarily it puts off the exercise of the call until as long as December. It is possible that the stock could drop below $50 by then, allowing you to either let the December 50 option expire or buy it back for less than the $7 you sold it for, keeping the difference. In either of these cases, you get to keep the underlying stock and not realize the taxes on the gain that you have in it.

This scenario does not allow you any more upside in the stock than the $50 call you already wrote in August, though it did give you $1,000 more premium overall and created a short term realized (and thus claimable for tax purposes) loss to offset gains. If you think that the stock has further to go, however, consider this:

Scenario 3a—Buy back August 50 call, sell December 55 call.

Action	Security	Shares	Options	Price	Net
Sold	August 50		5	$ 2	$1,000
Buy	August 50		-5	5	(2,500)
Sell	December 55		5	3.5	1,700
			TOTAL PROCEEDS:		$250

"Now", you ask, "why would I want to do that?" Your net overall profit on the calls is now only $250, compared to the $1,000 you had originally and the $2,000 you had in Scenario 2. Consider this—your new exercise price is $55, not $50, so if you do get called out on this option you will realize a gain of $5 more per share, or $2,500 overall, like this:

Scenario 3b—Buy back August 50 call, sell December 55 call, stock called at $55.

Action	Security	Shares	Options	Price	Net
Sold	August 50		5	$ 2	$1,000
Buy	August 50		-5	5	(2,500)
Sell	December 55		5	7	1,700
Sell	OW Stock	500		55	27,500
			TOTAL PROCEEDS:		$27,750

Not only that, but you have now created the same $1,500 capital loss with the buyback of your original August 50 options, which might be deductible versus capital gains.

These scenarios are only a sample of the ways you can work with covered calls to give you cash in your pocket while others speculate with your money. If your stock goes down, you keep the premiums, creating a nice hedge. If the stock rises, you are faced with the choice of selling it at a price that is likely higher than where it was trading when you began to consider the hedge. Alternatively, you can extend your options in hope of a pull-back in the stock (which would allow you to buy them back or simply allow them to expire).

One other aspect of using covered calls involves a bet that the underlying stock will go down or, put simply, a deferral of the sale of your stock. If you are quite bearish on a given stock holding, but for some reason do not want to actually sell it yet for tax or other reasons, you can write an in the money call option, or an option that has a strike price below the current market price of the stock.

For example, let's assume it's August and the stock is at $55 (we haven't sold any options previously for this scenario). You decide that the stock has nowhere to go but down, but aren't ready to sell it right now for some reason. The December 45 call option is trading at around $12 ($10 intrinsic value plus assumed $2 time premium), so you sell that option contract.

Scenario 4a—Sell in the money call when stock is at $55, stock is called out at $45 in December.

Action	Security	Shares	Options	Price	Net
Sell	December 45		5	$12	$ 6,000
Sell	OW Stock	500		45	22,500
			TOTAL PROCEEDS:		**$28,500**

The above example shows you being called out with total proceeds of $28,500 if the stock is anywhere above $45 at expiration, $1,000 more than you would have received selling at $55 today. However, if you are right and the stock drops below 45, things might look like this.

Scenario 4b—Sell in the money call when stock is at $55, stock falls below strike price.

Action	Security	Shares	Options	Price	Net
Sell	December 45		5	$ 12	$ 6,000
Buy	December 45		-5	1	(500)
			TOTAL PROCEEDS:		**$5,500**

In this case, the option has only minimal (I used $1) value as it approaches expiration, since the stock has fallen below the $45 strike. You could buy it back or simply let the expiration date come and go and not even pay for the buyback. Regardless, you have made a profit on the call option trade, which just happens to offset the unrealized loss in your stock. Most importantly, you still own your stock. If it rises again, you can sell it at a higher price or write another call, making money on the way down and on the way up. If you simply sell the stock today at around the $45 level, the net money you realize overall won't be all that different than if you had sold the stock when it was $55.

In the money calls can be useful as hedges in declining markets but also as a tax deferral mechanism. If it's almost a new tax year (say, November 30) but you don't want any more capital gains this year, you could sell an in the money call for a month in the next year. Unless the stock drops by quite a bit (in which case you are hedged as described above), you can allow yourself to be called out next year, essentially locking in today's price but not selling your stock until next year.

I could spend even more pages on variations of covered call strategies, but with some imagination you can come up with what will work best in your situation. The key to remember is that covered calls carry the cost of opportunity lost if your stock rises exponentially. You can do the extension trades as we outlined above, and eventually the stock may pull back enough so that you can close out the position and keep your stock. However, there is no guarantee that it will ever do so, and you may eventually just have to sell the stock for the strike price of the current option you have written.

Collars to protect yourself from dogs

For an investor who is using stock as collateral (for a home, a loan, or in a highly leveraged margin account) a collar is a low cost strategy which combines a married put and a covered call to limit the effect of fluctuations in the stock value. This is a good strategy for those who have concentrated stock positions which make up a large portion of your net worth. You might get this from a company stock plan, inheritance, or similar situation. Basically, if the stock ever turns into a dog and goes south, you are not exposed to the loss because you have a married put in place to hedge any loss. However, if you are buying married puts on an ongoing basis you probably do not want to spend the money on a new put option every few months. As we discussed, insurance can get expensive.

A solution? Sell a call to generate the cash to buy your put. For example, let's assume that a stock is at $50 and that people are generally ambivalent about its direction, making the calls and puts fairly evenly priced. A collar might look like this:

Action	Security	Shares	Options	Price	Net
Sold	December 55 call		5	$ 3	$ 1,500
Buy	December 45 put		-5	3	(1,500)
			TOTAL NET:		**$ 0**

Basically, your stock position is now in a "collar" until December, since if it falls you can "put" (sell) it at $45, but if it rises you will be called out at $55. Of course, if the market is excited about this stock you may sell the call for more than the put, and vice versa if the market is bearish. The stock will also seldom be at exactly the midway point between the two options, so the strike price which is closer to the market price will probably cost more since it would appear to be a more likely outcome at that time. It pays to examine several available ways of creating a collar to see which is most useful for your purposes. For larger positions ($1 million or more in principal), many investment banks can create a "synthetic" version of this and other transactions like it that are customized to your needs in terms of expiration, strike price, and profit/cost on the trade, et cetera.

Shorting

9

In the stock market, you can hold stock in an account—long or short. Most of us are very familiar with stock held long, since when you buy a stock you are by definition long in the account. You stay this way until you sell it sometime in the future. For a majority of investors, this is the only way they will trade stock. First, they will buy the stock, and sometime later they will sell the stock. Ideally, you will buy at a low price and sell at a high price.

However, there is a way to reverse the order of these transactions, which will result in a short position. If you sell a stock first, then buy it later, you are "short" the stock during the interim. Why would you sell a stock that you didn't own in the first place? The answer is simple: you believe that it will go down. You are simply trying to do the same thing as usual, but in reverse. Instead of "buy low, sell high," you are hoping to "sell high, buy low."

The other option is to be short in your account. There are certain arrangements which must be made with your brokerage before selling short. You must have enough cash or other assets available to allow you to actually purchase the stock that you are going to short, in case you are wrong and it rises. There is a cost associated with short positions as well, since the brokerage can't simply allow you to sell stock when you don't have any shares in your account. Shares must be borrowed in order to deliver shares to the party that buys when you are selling. Since this is a loan of sorts, you will probably be charged a fee or interest for selling short.

Shorting can also carry significant risks. If you sell a stock short you are betting that it will decline and you will be able to buy it back cheaper and pocket the difference. However, what happens if it goes up instead? You can experience a major loss if you don't "cover" the stock very quickly. (When you either deliver shares to the brokerage or buy the stock back in the market you have closed or covered the short position.)

For example, if you sell 500 shares of ABC short at $50, you could make quite a bit of money it if falls.

Sold 500 shares ABC short at $50. Stock then falls to $30, and 500 shares are purchased at $30 to "cover" short position.

	Shares	Price	Net
Short sale	500	$50	$25,000
Repurchase	500	30	(15,000)
		Profit:	$10,000

However, the risk of loss is technically unlimited, since the most a stock can go down is to zero, but it can rise (at least in theory) indefinitely. If the stock had instead risen to $70 and you had sold short at $50, you would experience a loss.

Obviously, you do not want to enact a short sale in your portfolio until you completely understand its uses and risks.

How can shorting help you hedge? There are several strategies, but we'll discuss the two most popular and leave your imagination to come up with others which might suit your needs.

Sold 500 shares ABC short at $50, stock then rises to $70; 500 shares purchased at $70 to "cover" short position.

	Shares	Price	Net
Short sale	500	$50	$25,000
Repurchase	500	70	(35,000)
		Loss:	($10,000)

Short against the box

Going short generally means selling a stock which you do not own, then hopefully buying shares in the open market at a lower price later on to deliver to the party (usually a brokerage) that you borrowed the first batch from. In the example of in the money calls, we were trying to either defer a sale or bet against the stock in the short term. A "short against the box" transaction has the same basic effect, though it does not use options to accomplish it. (I should note that as I am writing there is a legislation pending which would attempt to do away with this strategy as a means to defer capital gains taxes. Consult your tax advisor before enacting this or any other strategy which is meant to accomplish that goal.) The word box refers to a long position of shares which you already own.

Let's assume that you have 1,000 shares of Widgets of America Holdings (ticker symbol WOAH), which is an upstart competitor of Occidental Widget. You want to lock in today's price, but don't want to actually sell the stock yet. Let's say that WOAH is trading at $25 per share. To create a short against the box transaction, you will need to first borrow 1,000 shares of WOAH from your brokerage. This can be done in most non-retirement investment accounts.

You will then sell those 1,000 shares "short," meaning that you are selling a borrowed position, not one you actually own. But in actuality you do own 1,000 shares, right? Yes, but the brokerage can keep the two positions segregated until you tell them to "cover" the short position, meaning that they will deliver the long shares to cancel out the short position. Until this happens, your account will look like this:

Position	Security	Shares	Price	Net
Long	WOAH	1,000	$25	$25,000
Sold Short	WOAH	-1,000	25	(25,000)
			TOTAL NET:	**$0**

Now, what happens if the price goes down? Let's assume that it drops to $15 per share.

Position	Security	Shares	Price	Net
Long	WOAH	1,000	$25	$25,000
Current Value	WOAH	1,000	15	(15,000)
			TOTAL NET:	**$10,000**

Basically, since you realized a $25 price, you now have a choice to buy back stock in the open market to cover your short position, keeping the difference ($10 per share) and also leaving your original 1,000 shares of long stock untouched. Alternatively, you can at any time deliver your long shares to close the transaction that way, at which time you will have to recognize the gain on your 1,000 original shares based on your cost basis for those shares.

Of course, if the stock rises and it doesn't appear likely that it will fall back below where you sold it short, you should deliver the long shares and close the transaction as soon as it makes sense to do so. There is nothing to be gained in such a scenario, since you have effectively sold the stock at $25 already.

Short a competitor

Another interesting strategy involves buying your favorite company and selling short shares of a company which you think is a weak competitor. In theory, and often in practice, this serves to hedge against market fluctuations in the specific business sector which both companies are in. Essentially, this strategy is a long term bet that one company is the strongest competitor in its market. You hope your net return will be the degree of its outperformance versus the shorted company.

Let's assume that you think Widgets of America Holdings (WOAH) doesn't stand much of a chance against the giant, Occidental Widgets (OW). You want to own OW, but you are nervous that the widget sector may experience some serious upheaval if new regulations pass which mandate that the following warning label be placed on all widgets:

> This widget is not designed to be placed in your ear when activated; government testing has demonstrated that those who insist on doing so despite common knowledge that this is stupid may experience severe pain, loss of brain cells, and allergic reactions. This widget should not be used by drunks, fools, or those who lack common sense. Furthermore, there is a molecule in this widget which is known to the State of California to cause cancer when injected repeatedly in massive doses for decades on end into genetically inbred lab rats.

To own OW but still protect yourself from the potential problems in the industry, you decide to buy 500 shares of OW at $50 and sell short 1,000 shares of WOAH at $25. So, your account looks like this:

Position	Security	Shares	Price	Net
Long	OW	500	$50	$25,000
Sold Short	WOAH	-1,000	25	(25,000)
			TOTAL NET:	**$0**

Let's suppose that your concerns about the widget industry were right. The expense to relabel all of the millions of widgets puts a huge strain on the cost structure of all widget makers, and almost every stock in the sector begins to fall. Both OW and WOAH lose 20%, making your portfolio look like this:

Position	Security	Shares	Price	Net	
Long	OW	500	$50	$25,000	
Current Value	OW	500	40	20,000	
				NET:	**($5,000)**
Sold Short	WOAH	1,000	$25	$25,000	
Current Value	WOAH	1,000	20	20,000	
				NET:	**$5,000**

If you bought 1,000 shares of WOAH to cover the short, you would realize a gain of $5,000 and still maintain a long position of 500 shares of OW for the hopeful recovery. You would have effectively hedged the short term downward movement experienced by the widget sector. Otherwise, your net profit and loss will be zero.

But what if your fear about the effect of the warning labels was unfounded? Let's suppose that the warning labels only serve to make teenagers curious about what the big hubbub is about. Suddenly, teenagers everywhere begin doing exactly what the warning labels tell them not to do. They buy thousands of widgets to try putting them in their ears with their friends when their parents aren't looking. A huge widget fad sends sales flying for all the manufacturers, and all of their stocks rise 25%, making your portfolio look like this:

Position	Security	Shares	Price	Net	
Long	OW	500	$50	$25,000	
Current Value	OW	500	62.50	31,250	
				NET:	**$6,250**
Sold Short	WOAH	1,000	$25	$25,000	
Current Value	WOAH	1,000	31.25	31,250	
				NET:	**($6,250)**
				TOTAL NET:	**$0**

As you can see, if the stocks rise or fall in concert to the same degree, they essentially cancel each other out—you have a $6,250 gain on OW and a $6,250 loss on WOAH. So, the key to success in using this hedge strategy is to successfully choose the company which will outperform the rest of the sector.

Since OW is much larger and has better manufacturing capacity, the widget fad is no problem for them. They bring their production lines up to full capacity and make an extra ten million widgets in short order, capitalizing on the fad and making record sales. Their earnings look great, and the stock rises 50% in only a few months. WOAH, on the other hand, is a younger company and has to scramble to meet demand. They only produce a few more widgets in time to catch the sales boom, and though sales increase, they lose market share. WOAH stock rises a measly 5%. In this case, the strategy works:

Position	Security	Shares	Price	Net	
Long	OW	500	$50	$25,000	
Current Value	OW	500	75	37,500	
				NET:	**$12,500**
Sold Short	WOAH	1,000	$25	$25,000	
Current Value	WOAH	1,000	26.25	26,250	
				NET:	**($1,250)**
			TOTAL NET:		**$11,250**

In an ideal situation, the weaker competitor actually falls while the stronger gains, compounding your gains. Assuming OW gains 50% and WOAH drops 25%, your position would look like this:

Position	Security	Shares	Price	Net	
Long	OW	500	$50	$25,000	
Current Value	OW	500	75	37,500	
				NET:	**$12,500**
Sold Short	WOAH	1,000	$25	$25,000	
Current Value	WOAH	1,000	18.75	18,750	
				NET:	**$6,250**
			TOTAL NET:		**$18,750**

You get to cover your short position at a profit since WOAH fell after you sold it short, while keeping your profit on the stock that gained! Unfortunately, this strategy is not perfect, because you must be right about which company in the sector will be the leader. If you are wrong, remember that your account will look similar to the last example—except you will be short the stock that went up and long the one that went down, compounding your loss.

Over time, due to normal market fluctuations, you may be able to close the short on a downtrend and sell the long position on an uptrend, mitigating most of the mistake. However, especially in less developed industries, you can get caught in a vicious trap using this strategy if you essentially bet on the competitor which turns out to be the weaker of the two, so it is generally appropriate only in more mature market sectors unless you are willing to take a significant risk of loss in order to maximize your gain. Also, your brokerage may charge you interest on the position which you sell, which can add up to a substantial cost if you maintain the position for some time. Use shorting only if you understand it perfectly.

• • • • • • • •

The preceding few chapters should give you a basic picture of how you might hedge individual holdings. But what if you think that all of the companies in your portfolio are doing fine, but you are scared to death that a decade long bear market is about to descend upon us? Read on.

Fixed Returns

10

In earlier chapters I demonstrated that the stock market has provided historically superior returns versus other asset classes. This is true, and portfolio allocations should be made accordingly. However, many investors ignore certain parts of their portfolio which may determine a significant portion of their eventual wealth.

I'll use "fixed returns" to describe the income or gain you earn on certain investments that are generally predictable from year to year. Examples are common stock dividends, preferred stocks, CDs, bonds, and annuity payments. Equity (stock) markets do not rise indefinitely, and a well structured portfolio will have at least some portion of its assets in fixed return investments. Younger investors will want a much smaller fixed return component, since they can afford to risk more capital and may not want the income which fixed return investments provide. An investor who is near retirement will want a larger fixed return component, since she will need to be able to predict the value of the portfolio with a greater degree of certainty.

I should note that fixed return does not necessarily equate with stable prices or investment value. In some cases, the price of the investment itself may fluctuate, but the payment itself does not. For instance, if a stock pays a $1 dividend per share each year and you own 100 shares, you should receive a payment of $100 that year. The stock price itself may have gone from $10 to $25 and back down to $15, but the amount of your dividend payment stayed constant. Bonds also fluctuate in price, which I'll discuss later in this chapter.

It pays to be aware of the fixed return component of your portfolio, as some of the examples in this chapter will demonstrate. First we'll look at the bond market and how to use bonds in your portfolio. Then, we'll look at the long term effects of stock dividends in a portfolio.

Making zeros add up to more than nothing

One of the classic ways to gain a fixed income position in your portfolio, especially tax deferred accounts where you can avoid taxation of income, is to buy a zero coupon bond position. These can mature when you may need the money for retirement, college, or they can have a laddered structure to allow you to take advantage of changes in interest rates over time. We'll discuss ladder and barbell structures used (to reduce volatility) at the end of this section.

First, however, a primer on how bonds, and especially zero coupon bonds, work. You will sometime see the words fixed income and bonds used synonymously. Fixed income investments actually encompass a much broader range of investments. I'm going to refer to bonds as a generic term for U.S. Treasury bonds, since then we can deal with only the basic concepts without confusing things with the variables of credit quality, investment ratings, and bond types, which enter into the behavior of the corporate and municipal bond markets. If you are already familiar with the relationships between maturity, coupon, price, and yield, then skip ahead a few paragraphs. Here are some basic definitions:

Maturity refers to the date in the future that the issuer of the bond will pay back the principal of the bond in cash. All normal bonds have a par value of $1,000 at maturity. If you invest $10,000 in a bond which matures on July 15, 2005, you will receive $10,000 back on that date. In the interim, you will be earning interest on the bond.

A bond's **coupon** is the interest it pays each year, expressed as a percentage of its par value. So, a bond which has a 6% coupon pays $60 per year to its owner (6% of $1,000). Important: remember that coupon is not the same as yield, though both may be expressed as a percentage.

A bond's **price** is determined by the market between issue and maturity, and is a function of the bond's coupon, quality, and maturity date. Most bonds (with the notable exception of zeroes, which we'll discuss) are issued for $1,000 and come due at $1,000 per bond. The value at maturity is called the bond's par value. However, bonds do trade between the time they are issued and their maturity dates (As a matter of fact, the dollar volume in the bond market is much larger than the stock market each day). To explain why prices fluctuate, consider this.

Pretend that you bought a bond which paid a 7% coupon ($70 per year) for $1,000 two years ago. Since that time, however, the best coupon you can find on new bonds of the same maturity is 5% ($50 per year), because interest rates have dropped. If you went to sell your first bond, you might notice that it was worth more than what you paid. This is because if the bonds available today are only paying $50 per year, that $70 per year payment looks more valuable. Your bond might be worth $1,400 now, which would put its return in line with the current 5% coupons investors have available to them.

Two years ago, you bought a bond with a coupon of 7%, or $70 per year. Interest rates drop, and new bonds are being issued with coupons for 5%, or $50 per year.

Your bond	
"Par" Value	$1,000
Coupon	7.00%
Annual Income	$70.00

New bonds being issued	
"Par" value	$1,000
Coupon	5.00%
Annual Income	$50.00

Value of your bond, to equate to a 5% coupon yield on newly issued bonds.

"Par" Value	$1,000
Annual Income	$70.00
Current Yields	5.00%
Trading price of 7% bond to equal currend yield:	$1,400

This return for a buyer at today's price is the **yield** on the bond. If your 7% coupon bond is now worth $1,400, it has a simple yield of 5% to anyone who buys it from you. This is because $70 divided by $1,400 is .05, or 5%. Bond prices, and hence yields, are always changing as traders bet on the direction of the economy and Federal Reserve activity by watching and reacting to every minuscule piece of economic data.

Incidentally, bonds are quoted as a percent of par ($1,000), so a bond selling for "98 1/2" will cost you $985, and a bond quoted at "105" is worth $1,050. This is important to remember to avoid confusion.

As a basic rule, remember that bond prices and yields are like a teeter totter, when one rises, the other falls, and vice versa.

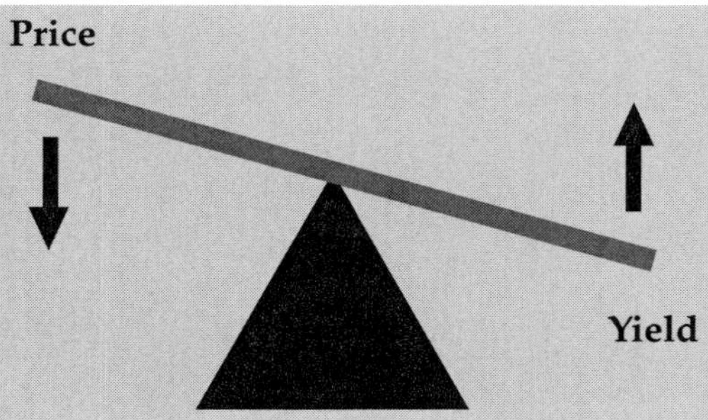

Now, let's move to a specific kind of bond: the zero coupon bond. The yield on a zero coupon bond may be similar to that of a regular bond of similar maturity, but zero coupon bonds have two very important differences from regular bonds:

A zero trades at a discount to its par value because its coupon, or the amount of interest it pays each year, is zero. So, instead of being issued at $1,000, paying coupon payments each year, then maturing at $1,000, a zero coupon bond is issued at less than $1,000, pays no interest, but still matures at $1,000. The difference between issue price and the maturity value is your rate of return. A bond sold for $500 which matures in ten years for $1,000 has a rate of about 7.19% compound annual yield. To quickly find out how long it will take to double your money at a given rate of return, use the "rule of 72." Divide the number 72 by your rate of return and you will come very close to the exact period of time it will take for your money to double at that rate. For instance, a 7.2% compounded rate of return will double your money in 10 years, a 9% rate will double your money in eight years (72 divided by 9 equals 8), and an 12% rate will double your money in six years (72 divided by 12 equals 6).

Because zeroes do not pay any interest they are more volatile and responsive to changes in the market. Thus, a zero is an investment that in the worst case you can hold to maturity and earn the yield calculated by the amount of discount you paid when you bought it. However, if rates fall (and hence prices rise), you can sell it at a profit. Let's look at a scenario in this regard.

You buy ten U.S. Treasury zero coupon bonds, which mature in 20 years at $1,000 apiece. Current rates for that maturity are 6.95%, so the bonds are selling at 25.5, or $255 per bond. So, worst case, you will earn 6.95% per year, compounded for the next 20 years if you hold the bonds to maturity. But what if rates drop sometime between now and maturity? Here's an example of this market action's effect on the above bond:

TODAY:
Bought 10M
0% coupon
10/15/17maturity @ $255
Yield 6.95%

Let's assume that one year later the yields on new bonds with maturities nineteen years away are 6% (remember, one year has passed, so our twenty year maturity is now down to nineteen). Since this bond will be worth something in line with what investors can get in the current market, you will make a profit of more than 27% in the relative price of the bond:

ONE YEAR LATER:
Sell 10M
0%coupon
10/15/17maturity @ $325.22
Yield 6%

If you believe that the bond market run up (thus moving yields lower) is only temporary, you can sell the bond and capture the gain and (hopefully) buy another similar bond if rates rise to attractive levels again. Remember, though, one of the risks of selling a bond after a good gain is that there may be few places to invest at a rate of return that you are used to, since rates will have fallen.

But what if rates rise? Bond prices will fall, but on the bright side, a bond will inexorably march towards its $1,000 maturity value, so the closer to that maturity date you are the less volatile the bond will be.

The longer the maturity, the lower the price of a zero coupon, since a zero pays no interest but has a yield based on its discount from par value. If a bond matures in one year at $1,000, a $950 price gives about 5.2% return when it matures, but a ten year zero would have a price of $597.29 to yield the same 5.2% per year for those ten years.

Two common ways to decrease the overall volatility of a bond portfolio are structures called ladders and barbells. In a laddered bond portfolio, you divide your funds among bonds which mature at staggered times. For instance, let's assume that it's the fall of 1997, and you have $100,000 to invest in bonds. Instead of buying a 20 year maturity, zero coupon bond yielding 6.5%, you buy about $10,000 worth of each of the following zero coupon bonds.

Maturity	Price	#Bonds	Net $	Yield
11/15/98	$69.00	14	$ 9,660	5.50%
11/15/99	57.50	17	9,775	5.60%
11/15/00	52.00	19	9,880	5.75%
11/15/02	46.00	22	10,120	5.95%
11/15/04	40.00	25	10,000	6.04%
11/15/07	36.00	28	10,080	6.08%
11/15/12	35.00	29	10,150	6.11%
11/15/17	32.00	31	9,920	6.25%
11/15/22	28.00	36	10,080	6.34%
11/15/27	25.20	40	10,080	6.50%
Cash			255	
		TOTAL:	$100,000	
		WEIGHTED AVERAGE YIELD:	6.00%	
		TOTAL AT MATURITY:	**$261,000**	

Note that you get a substantial part of the yield on the single 20 year bond position while experiencing much less volatility since the bonds on the short end of the ladder are continuously coming due and being reinvested at current market rates. The portfolio will roll forward over time, effectively averaging you in and out of the market. If you want to own bonds long term as opposed to trading them as described above, this can be an attractive strategy.

A similar strategy involves buying bonds with long maturities and bonds with short maturities, with the expectation that the long bonds will give higher yield while the shorter ones will be reinvested on a continual basis and provide a low volatility way to average in and out of the market. This strategy is often referred to as a "barbell," and it can make sense when the yields on the longer bonds are significantly higher or lower than the rates on shorter bonds.

Maturity	Price	#Bonds	Net $	Yield
11/15/98	$69.00	29	$ 20,010	5.50%
11/15/99	57.50	35	20,125	5.60%
11/15/00	34.00	59	20,060	5.60%
11/15/22	28.00	71	19,880	6.45%
11/15/27	25.20	79	19,908	6.75%
Cash			17	
		TOTAL:	$100,000	
		WEIGHTED AVERAGE YIELD:	5.98%	
		TOTAL AT MATURITY:	**$273,000**	

Again, the goal is to structure the portfolio to offer the maximum yield potential and flexibility with the minimum amount of risk/volatility if the portfolio is meant to be held and traded only as bonds come due.

Incidentally, the first thing the Federal Reserve did after the crash of 1987 was to lower short term interest rates to make more money available to stimulate the economy and the stock market. The bond market usually follows the trend set by the Federal Reserve, so this strengthened bond prices almost immediately. Those who truly understand the market know that the bond market rules the world of investments.

Dividends

There is a well known and increasingly popular strategy which involves buying the top dividend yielding stocks of the Dow, holding them for one year, then repeating the process and holding only the stocks that pass the screening process at that time. There are many variations on the strategy—some recommend buying the top five, others the top ten; some reallocate the portfolio monthly, others yearly. Others use further criteria and formulas to attempt to squeeze out an extra percent or two.

However, all of the "Dow Dividend" strategies have one thing in common—dividends. It is said that if ignorance paid dividends, everyone would make a fortune in the stock market. It does not, of course, so those who take the time to think through their investments will finish ahead.

It doesn't take a leap of logic to realize that if the market gets scared, securities which pay a return in good times and bad will suddenly become much more popular on a relative basis. If everything seems to be crashing, most stocks will probably do the same, in the short term.

If your hot growth stock falls 50%, say from $20 to $10, you are left with an unrealized loss of $10 per share, some angst, and the fervent hope that the stock will rise to do justice to the great fundamentals that you just know are still present in the underlying company. Now, say you own a stock identical to this example, except that it pays a 5% dividend which you wisely put on automatic dividend reinvestment.

Now assume that this stock falls from $20 to $10. There are probably going to be some marked differences between the long term performance of the two. Number one, since the price has fallen in half, the same dividend is now 10% of the stock price. ($1 divided by $20 stock price is 5%, but the same $1 divided by a $10 stock price is 10%.) In a falling market, that may seem quite attractive to money managers seeking safe havens, and may serve to stabilize its price long before other stocks which offer no ongoing return unless their prices are rising. Second, though you still feel some angst, that dividend may make you feel a little better (especially if it is in a tax deferred account such as an IRA, SEP, or other qualified plan).

Let's assume we buy the same $20 stock, which falls to $10 shortly after the purchase, but recovers by $2 per year after that. The difference to your net worth when we look at the effect of the dividend after even a few years makes the value of that little 5% quite apparent. Note that for this illustration, we used quarterly dividend reinvestment, though we artificially assumed that the stock stayed the same price throughout the year, then went up $2 at the end of each year for five years. (See Example 1 on the following page.)

Example 1

Year	1	2	3	4	5	6	7	8	9	10
Current Price	$10.00	12.00	14.00	16.00	18.00	20.00	20.00	20.00	20.00	20.00
Total dividend	$1.00	1.00	1.00	1.00	1.00	1.00	1.00	1.00	1.00	1.00
Dividend in %	10.0%	8.3%	7.1%	6.3%	5.6%	5.0%	5.0%	5.0%	5.0%	5.0%
Beginning shares	1,000.00	1,103.81	1,205.47	1,305.54	1,404.4	1,502.29	1,599.41	1,697.83	1,797.57	1,898.66
Shares purchased	103.81	101.65	100.07	98.86	97.9	97.11	98.42	99.75	101.09	102.45
Ending shares	1,103.81	1,205.47	1,305.54	1,404.4	1,502.29	1,599.41	1,697.83	1,797.57	1,898.66	2,001.11
Net cost basis	19.06	18.46	18.12	17.97	17.97	18.1	18.21	18.31	18.4	18.48
Net value	$11,038	$14,466	$18,278	$22,470	$27,041	$31,988	$33,957	$35,951	$37,973	$40,022

Example 2

Year	1	2	3	4	5	6	7	8	9	10
Current Price	$10.00	12.00	14.00	16.00	18.00	20.00	20.00	20.00	20.00	20.00
Shares	1,000	1,000	1,000	1,000	1,000	1,000	1,000	1,000	1,000	1,000
Overall value	$10,000	$12,000	$14,000	$16,000	$18,000	$20,000	$20,000	$20,000	$20,000	$20,000

Now, refer to Example 2 and let's see what happens if the stock pays no dividend, but still rises the same amount in price

I would say that the difference ($20,022, or more than 100%) is worth considering. The dividend that seemed insignificant when you bought the stock at $20 can become quite significant over time. Even better, try to find companies which have consistently raised their dividends year after year.

There are plenty of them out there, and even a small regular increase in the dividend makes a tremendous amount of difference to the long term investor over a period of years. A 3% rise in the dividend (say, from $1 to $1.03 per year) will logically translate into a 3% rise in the stock if every other condition in the market remains the same. Of course, no other condition in the market remains the same for more than a minute or two, but relative value is obviously added by a larger dividend. Additionally, a good track record of rising dividends will make investors take a look at the stock as a safe haven in volatile times.

Bored MBAs

11

When MBAs get bored on Wall Street, they go to little rooms filled with brilliant techno-wizards using supercomputers deep in the guts of skyscrapers. Together they scheme, manipulate, and use alchemistry to produce strange new creatures like TIGRS, MITTS, MIPPS, QUIPS, ELKS, and even LYONS! This is probably starting to sound like sub-Saharan Africa or a zoo, both of which actually have a lot in common with Wall Street. But that could be the subject of another book entirely.

All of these acronyms were invented by Wall Street firms to describe derivative products that offer some twist on the basic stocks, bonds, and funds that we are used to dealing with. Some offer tax advantages for companies which issue stocks and bonds, others protect your principal while allowing you to track an index, and others are simply options with extra long maturities. Derivatives will always exist, with new ones being created constantly, limited only by the imaginations of the aforementioned highly compensated MBAs with megacomputers in Manhattan. Trust me, they have great imaginations.

Converting gains

A type of defensive holding not mentioned in the previous chapter are bonds or preferred stock which are convertible into stock. These can combine some of the advantages of equity (stocks) and debt (bonds) into a single security. That is, you may receive a higher dividend or interest payment than you would had you owned the common shares of the same company, while retaining at least a portion of the underlying stock's growth potential.

There are endless variations of these securities. More are created as we discover new ways to arrange things to maximize tax and other benefits to the issuing company while making the securities more attractive to buyers. A small sampling of these securities is listed in Appendix E. For now, just remember that most bonds and preferred stocks pay a fixed rate of return, though naturally there are exceptions to that rule as well.

For the same reasons that stocks with high dividend yields are an interest paying security is inherently more defensive than an equity (stock). Bonds have a maturity date in the future at which the issuing company repays the loan you made to it by buying its bond. Preferred stocks are a hybrid of sorts between common stock and a bond; while they usually pay a fixed rate of return, they may have no maturity (perpetual), a very long maturity (2020 and beyond is not unusual), and/or a call feature that allows the issuing company to redeem your stock at a fixed price on certain dates. However, they also usually lack the voting and certain other rights of a common stock.

A normal bond or preferred stock does not offer the growth potential that the common stock of the same issuing company might. This is because their price is based on the promise that they will pay a certain return for a certain time and then return your principal. Your eventual return is based solely on their ability to repay that debt, and you will not necessarily participate in the long term fortunes of the company outside of their hopeful future solvency.

There are, however, certain types of bonds and preferred stocks which are convertible into common stock, giving you a little of both worlds. If you buy carefully, this can be an excellent way to buy a company you like but limit your risk. There are literally thousands of convertible stocks and bonds. Generally, most brokerages can provide you information about what has been issued by a given company, and a good stock and bond guide will contain listings of convertibles.

Let's use the history of a recently converted preferred stock as an example of how one might work. RJR Nabisco (ticker "RN") issued preferred stock in May, 1994. It was convertible at a ratio of 5:1 into the common stock of the company on May 15, 1997. Each year until that time, however, the preferred would pay a dividend of 15¢ per quarter. With an issue price of $6.50, this was an annual yield of 9.2%, compared to about 6.5% on the common stock. The preferred stock was called RJR Nabisco preferred class C (ticker "RNprC"). Companies with more than one issue of preferred stock outstanding assign letters to differentiate them.

	Price on 5/15/94	Quarterly Dividend	Yield (Dvd/Price)	Conversion Ratio
Common stock (RN)	$30.00	0.406	5.41%	1
Preferred convertible stock (RNprC)	$6.50	0.150	9.23%	5

Even though RNprC was not going to convert into the common stock for several years, it moved in concert with the underlying common stock because of the fact that it would eventually convert. The market is very efficient about calculating the effect of such things, though occasionally you can find a rare opportunity when a convertible is trading at a discount to its conversion price, which RNprC did do a few times in its life.

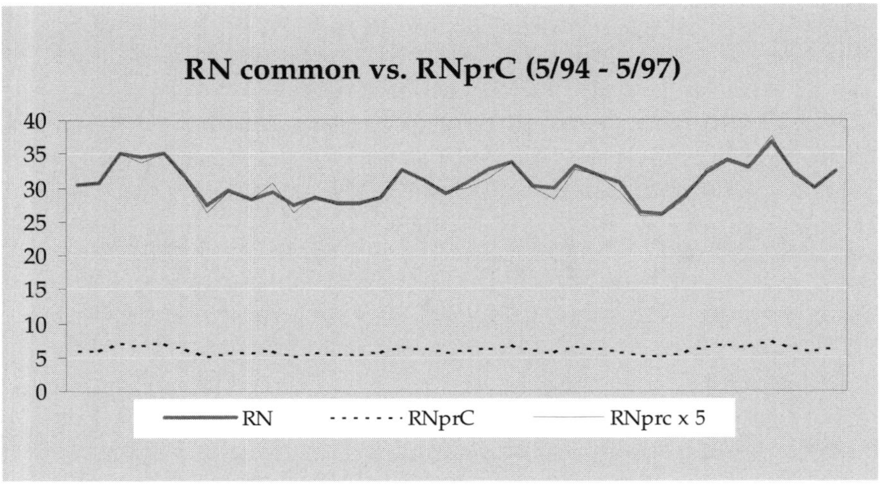

Why buy the convertible instead of the common stock? In this case, the dividend on the preferred was much higher than that of the common. This provided both a better overall return over the life of the security and some measure of downside protection since you would still receive a hefty dividend even when the price of your stock was falling.

Conversions can happen in various ways. Some are mandated in the terms of the security. On May 15, 1997, the preferred will convert to common stock at a ratio of 5 shares of preferred class C to one share of common stock." Others are convertible anytime at the discretion of the holder, the company, or either. Event clauses will also sometimes trigger a conversion, such as "in the event that the company is merged with or taken over by another company, the preferred shares will immediately convert to common stock."

Some things to be aware of in preferred stocks are features like cumulative monthly income, and those which are issued by foreign companies. A cumulative clause means that if the company does not pay dividends on their preferred stock as scheduled, they must in the future pay back all of the dividends in arrears before paying off certain other creditors or spending money in other ways. Monthly income preferreds do just what the name implies—instead of paying your dividends each quarter or semiannually, they are divided up into smaller pieces that are paid monthly. While there are many foreign companies which issue preferred convertible stocks in the U.S., it pays to be aware that sometimes there is a mandatory tax withholding that is taken out when the dividend is paid. However, in many cases that taxation can be reclaimed when you do your taxes, so it is mostly just an inconvenience unless you have a complex financial situation.

Convertible bonds are similar to preferred stock in behavior but not structure. Unlike the preferred stock, a convertible bond usually has a fixed, shorter maturity. It is not uncommon for preferreds to come due fifty years in the future (In reality, a majority of preferreds have call features which allow the issuers to buy your stock from you at a set price starting on a stated date in the future. It is rare that a preferred stock makes it all the way to maturity unless it is a very cheap source of financing for the issuer).

If a company goes bankrupt and becomes subject to liquidation, certain securities are more senior than others, and the holders of those securities must be paid before those who are next in line. The bonds may be in a senior position to a preferred stock, though most preferreds are senior to common stock. It is worthwhile to do some research and find out where your holding stands in the pecking order. If it is a strong company it may not be as relevant as a more speculative holding that you are concerned may not have the ability to meet its obligations if something goes wrong.

One of the keys to investing in convertible securities is a thorough understanding of the concept of parity. Parity is basically the price at which the convertible stock becomes exactly equal to the price of the common stock if it were to be converted. For instance, if the RNprC convertible preferred were trading at $7 and the RN common stock were trading at $35, they would be trading at parity since the conversion terms were exactly 5:1. However, if the RNprC were trading at $7 but the common stock was at $30, the preferred would be trading at a premium to parity of approximately 16.7%. Here are some examples:

Terms of conversion, in shares

Common:	1
Preferred:	5

Common Price	Preferred Price	Preferred value if converted to common	Net above/(below) current price of common stock	Percentage difference
$40	$7	35	(5)	-12.50% discount
35	7	35	0	0.00% parity
30	7	35	5	16.67% premium
35	6	30	(5)	-14.29% discount
35	7	35	0	0.00% parity
35	8	40	5	14.29% premium

It is important to know the exact conversion terms of any such security, since some may be trading at a very significant premium to their conversion value. While this may not exclude the security from consideration (for instance, if the underlying stock has incredible growth possibilities), it should make you look at the relative value of owning it.

Arachnid allies

Many people would be very happy to simply match the ups and downs of the market over time, because those who have done so have made a lot of money on a fairly consistent basis. Unfortunately, the vast majority of individual investors and fund managers are not able to accomplish this. For this reason, so-called "index" funds have become increasingly popular recently as people seek to passively match the performance of the index.

Unfortunately, the overwhelming majority of index funds (and most other equity funds as well) underperform the return on the indexes they seek to track.

If you managed a $500 million index fund that was supposed to perform in line with the S&P 500, it would seem a simple task to do so—you would buy every stock in the index, or $1 million of each component of the S&P 500. Simple. So why the underperformance? There are many reasons.

First, any mutual fund must pay for employees, computers, advertising, sales support, record keeping, and even to send your monthly statement to you. All funds, even so-called "no load" funds, experience these expenses. Certain funds pay for some of those expenses by charging you a fee (or load) up front, and then often have lower ongoing expenses if you remain a long term holder of the fund.

Incidentally, there are several studies which show that the average investor in a loaded fund does better than the average investor in a no load fund that has an identical annual return. How is this the case? Consider this: which fund would you be more willing to trade in and out, one where you paid nothing to do so, or one where you had to pay a commission each time? This is just one more instance which demonstrates that timing the market seldom works over the long haul. Statistically, no load investors are more likely to try to time the market, while loaded fund owners just spend a lot of time in the market.

The second reason that index funds find it difficult to match their index is that the fund cannot be completely invested in stocks all the time. In open ended funds, investors are always taking money out and putting money in, often at exactly the wrong time. When the market has a major correction people tend to panic and pull their money out of the mutual fund, forcing the fund to sell off stocks (at low prices due to the correction) in order to raise money to send to these foolish traders. Then, at the bottom of the correction, when it would logically be a great time to buy, the fund has no money to get back into those stocks, because the average individual investor normally waits until the market has already risen (note past tense) before buying back in. No matter how hard an index fund tries to track its index, it will be an uphill battle even before the expenses are added in because the manager must keep at least some cash on hand for redemptions. This means not all the money is actually invested in the index.

So, if you want to match the index are you doomed to simply have to buy all the stocks in it? No. There are vehicles other than index funds which do this for you, but they are not mutual funds. They are not actively managed, have minimal expenses, and do not experience the flow of investor money in and out of the portfolio.

One of the most popular is called a "SPDR" (pronounced "spider" by traders), which stands for Standard & Poors Depository Receipt. These trade on the American Stock Exchange under the ticker "SPY," and each one represents one tenth of the price of the S&P 500. If the S&P is at 850, the SPDRs will be approximately $85, give or take a little depending on the mood of the market. Since a SPDR is actually backed by a trust containing the stocks of the S&P 500, you will receive the dividends and experience the price gains and losses of the stocks in the trust. You essentially own the index, with only minimal expenses.

As I write this, rumor has it that there will soon be a similar security based on the Dow Jones Industrial Average. It will trade on the American Stock Exchange and will be known as Diamond, with the ticker symbol DIA.

Another alternative can be found in defined asset funds, which are offered by most of the major brokerage houses. These funds (sometimes called Unit Investment Trusts) buy a group of stocks according to a predetermined screening process. They are not actively managed portfolios, but several of the screening strategies have consistently outperformed the broad markets. By far the most popular are the Dow Dividend strategies, in which the fund buys the top ten (or top five in some cases) dividend yielding stocks in the Dow Jones Industrial Average and holds them in a trust for one year or more.

Several firms also offer defined asset funds which hold stocks that are screened using other strategies: undervalued but still high quality stocks in the S&P, stocks which are the top picks of a firm's analysts, and utility stocks with above average growth rates, to name only a few. International stock portfolios are increasingly available in this form as well, with stocks being selected with similar dividends or other strategies.

These can be great vehicles to build a base for a portfolio without having to research or trade many individual stocks. However, I believe that a word of caution is in order when considering indexing. In our current market, I believe that the obsession with trying to keep up with the market averages has created problems of its own. There are tens of thousands of stocks on the various exchanges, but the indices are made up of a limited number—30 in the case of the Dow Jones Industrial Average, 500 in the S&P. These are the highest quality public companies in the opinion of most professionals. Similar to the Nifty 50 phenomena several decades ago, a comparably small group of these blue chip companies have been aggressively purchased by fund managers and other professional investors in recent years.

The process feeds upon itself, for as they are bid up others feel that they must buy these particular stocks in order to keep up with the indices (and competitor's investment performance). This simply pushes the prices higher again. The broader markets lag the blue chip indices, and investors begin moving out of their non-performing assets into the same stocks that everyone else is buying. This process cannot go on forever, of course. Eventually the market turns to fundamental analysis of relative value. When that happens, the stocks that have been the great performers look expensive. I believe that it may be the ninth inning for indexing. Then again, I might be wrong—the market has a way of defying rational thought for extended periods of time.

LEAPS in bondage

"Don't be afraid to take a big step if one is indicated; you can't cross a chasm in two small jumps."—Lloyd George

No, this book did not just take a very strange turn. What if you could capture most of the potential return on a given stock in a fixed time period, while exposing yourself to only a fraction of the risk? For instance, let's assume that you want to own General Contraptions Corporation (ticker TRAP) stock because of some major new initiatives the company has launched this year. However, although you have $10,000 to invest, you are nervous about what might happen if the company cannot execute their ambitious strategy.

Certain stocks have options with expirations well into future years. These very long options contracts are called LEAPS, which stands for Long-term Equity Anticipation Securities. To utilize the strategy discussed here, you must first find the LEAPS on the stock we are interested in buying. If it does not have LEAPS, find the longest expiration available in that stock's options. Note that LEAPS usually have a different symbol than the regular options for the stock. A list of popular stocks with LEAPS available is in Appendix B.

Incidentally, there are many theoretical measures of option valuation that can help you decide which option looks cheapest relative to the other strike prices and expirations. Though common sense will generally serve you well in this decision, I recommend that you get one of the many books on options trading. If you would like to learn more about valuation or get a patient broker who is well versed in options trading.

Let's say we find that General Contraptions has LEAPS which expires eighteen months from now. The stock is currently trading at $50, and you decide that the $60 LEAPS option looks like the best value. Your LEAPS is trading at $5, which seems like a lot since it has a strike price of $60, which is 10% over the current price of the stock. However, keep in mind that for the next year and a half you are getting all the upside of the stock in excess of $55, for about one tenth of the price you would pay to buy the stock outright.

So, you have $10,000 to spend. Normally, that would buy 200 shares of General Contraptions. To replace the upside you would experience in the stock you will have to buy options contracts representing at least 200 underlying shares. So, you buy two LEAPS options on General Contraptions, costing a total of $1,000 (2 x $500 per option). Now you have $9,000 of what you have to invest left over—what are you going to do with it? A popular strategy involves buying U.S. Treasury bonds or similar issues with a maturity matched to your LEAPS, like this:

Assuming purchase date of July 15, 1997

Issue	Quantity	Price	Net
TRAP January 1999 $55 call	2	$ 5	$ 1,000
U.S. Treasury 6% maturing 1/15/99	9	1,000	9,000
		TOTAL	$10,000

At expiration, several things may have happened. First, if the stock went down to $35, your portfolio looks like this:

Issue	Quantity	Price	Net
TRAP January 1999 $55 call	2	$ 0	$ 0
U.S. Treasury 6% maturing 1/15/99	9	1,000	9,000
Cash			810
		TOTAL	$9,810

Compare this to what would happen if you had just used your $10,000 to buy the 200 shares of stock—your holding would now be worth only $7,000 with the stock at $35. This strategy saved $2,810 over holding the stock itself. But, where did that extra cash come from? With a 6% rate on $9,000 of Treasury bonds for 18 months you have received $810 of interest payments. Incidentally, the above example holds true even if General Contraption (TRAP) dives down to nothing—since the options cannot be worth less than zero, the risk exposure to the stock is limited to the amount you invested in the options. So, worst case, you might lose just under 2% of your principal in this example.

Issue	Quantity	Price	Net
TRAP January 1999 $55 call	2	$ 15	$ 3,000
U.S. Treasury 6% maturing 1/15/99	9	1,000	9,000
Cash			810
		TOTAL	**$12,810**

But what if you were right, and the company's stock moves up to $70? With the stock at $70, if you had bought 200 shares they would be worth $14,000, for a gain of $4,000. However, using the bonded LEAPS strategy, you gained about $2,810. This is because the option is now worth the difference between the strike and the current price ($70 minus $55 equals $15) and you are earning interest on the bond regardless. This does not seem that impressive until you consider that at this price you have experienced more than 70% of the upside on the stock while being exposed to a negligible amount of downside. Moreover, the better the stock does, the higher your participation rate. Let's look at the portfolio again if General Contraptions is a real barn burner and goes all the way to $90 per share:

Issue	Quantity	Price	Net
TRAP January 1999 $55 call	2	$ 35	$ 7,000
U.S. Treasury 6% maturing 1/15/99	9	1,000	9,000
Cash			810
		TOTAL	**$16,810**

In this case, had you held 200 shares you would have gained $8,000 (200 x $90/share less the $10,000 original investment). With the bonded LEAPS strategy you made $6,810, experiencing over 85% of the upside. Again, you did this with only a tiny fraction of the potential downside of owning the stock outright.

When I talk to groups of investors, someone usually pipes up and asks why we don't just use the money we spent on bonds to buy other investments or leverage ourselves to effectively "buy" more shares of the targeted stock via LEAPS. My answer to this question may be unsatisfying to some, but I reply that this strategy creates discipline. I have seen many portfolios that start out to be conservative or defensive in nature turn quite speculative because we are all human. Options can be very powerful tools, and can leverage your capital to an incredible degree. With a few successes in using them human nature causes us to put more and more of our capital into what is working at the time. Unfortunately, the leverage works both ways, and the losses can be extreme.

Having a portfolio with a large call option component is not defensive in the least. I believe that options should be purchased only with money that you can afford to lose, since there is a major fundamental difference between options and the stocks they represent. If the underlying stock drops a few points after you buy a call option (or the stock rises after you buy a put option), that option may be completely worthless at expiration. The stock may have only dropped 10% had you owned it, but the option will have irretrievably lost 100% of its value. The stock may rise again someday and give your money back, but the option premium you paid is a final realized loss. The bonded LEAPS strategy insures that we do what we wanted to do—make money if our stock rises, but not experience significant loss if it falls. Basically, it protects us from our own nature by keeping our investments disciplined within the plan we set out.

The index options in the prior chapter can be used as well, since there are not only puts on the indices, but calls as well. Thus, you can track a majority of the gain in, for instance, the S&P 500, with a very limited amount of downside. To do so, you would go through the same process as we did for the General Contraptions options, except substitute a long S&P call option in the account.

Many stocks have related securities called warrants, which are similar in nature to LEAPS. A warrant is basically a call option issued by the company, often along with its stock as a "sweetener" to original investors or as part of a merger, acquisition, or other transaction. The warrant may have various terms, including strike prices and maturity dates. If you exercise a warrant to buy stock, however, a warrant is very different from an option in that you actually do buy the stock from the issuing company, instead of from the open market via an options exchange. It is worth finding out if a company you are considering buying has warrants, since warrants can be used in much the same way as a LEAPS to obtain upside without exposing yourself to the entire downside that may be present in the common stock. Generally, a warrant is traded on the same exchange as the common, and is denoted as a "W" or "ws" or another symbol after the primary stock symbol. For instance, Intel (INTC) has warrants which trade under the ticker symbol INTCW.

MITTS, or how to catch a line drive without breaking your portfolio

Wall Street has created products that seek to accomplish what we just described (capturing the potential gain on an index with principal protection) without having to buy an option at all. Several Wall Street firms offer trusts or funds which are guaranteed by the issuing company (or some other arrangement) to come due at a specified value in the future, plus whatever gain the related index makes in the same time. New securities of this type are becoming more and more popular as investors are concerned about the market's heights, yet want to remain invested.

A partial list of securities and funds with principal protection is in Appendix D, though I am sure that not all that exist are included. Ask your advisor for recommendations if this type of structure is attractive to you.

I'll use a recent issue as an example of how principal protected securities might work. On the New York Stock Exchange (NYSE) there is a stock that does not represent any company at all. Its ticker is MIM, its official moniker is MITTS (Market Index Target Term Security). Repayment of original principal is backed by one of the most established Wall Street firms. Five years after it was issued it will come due at $10, plus the percentage gain on the S&P 500 between its issue date and maturity. This particular security was issued when the S&P 500 was just over 800.

Let's assume that on September 16, 2002, the S&P has grown to 1,400 (a compound gain of around 12% per year). The 75% overall gain in the index will translate into a price of $17.50, equaling the $10 base plus $7.50, which you will receive in cash.

If the S&P is below 813.65 (the exact starting index value on this issue), you would simply receive your $10 back. If that should happen, your loss would be the opportunity cost of what you could have earned on your money elsewhere. That is a real risk and should not be taken lightly. If you do not believe that the market is a good place to be long term, then why not earn money market rates at least?

The exchange listed securities of this type are normally liquid just like a stock. This means that you can sell them any time before maturity for their market value. If the underlying index is up since issue, its approximate gain will probably be reflected in the security's price. However, because the payment for the movement of the market is in the future, securities of this type may not move exactly in line with the index short term.

Remember that most principal protected investments are only guaranteed to return the amount at which they were issued or some other stated value. If you buy MIM at $11, for example, you will receive any future growth in the security above your cost basis, but the only principal that is guaranteed to be returned at maturity is $10 per share, which was the original offering price and was pegged to the underlying index on the day of issue.

Recently, there have been trusts of this type issued which track the Japanese, Latin American, and European markets. Surely there are more coming, each with their own variations. There is even one which combines protection against rising inflation with partial participation in the S&P 500 index.

Certain of these issues have participation rates in excess of 100%. This means that they will participate in the growth of the underlying index to a larger degree than had you owned the index itself. A recent MITTS (ticker JEM on the NYSE) issue with the Japanese Nikkei as the underlying index has a participation rate of 140% and a par value of $10. So, if the Nikkei goes up 75% (or 15% per year) between the issue date and five year maturity, the firm that issued the securities will be obligated to pay $20.50 per share to all holders on that date. This is the $10 original issue price, plus 1.4 times the growth in the underlying index, which works out to an extra $10.50 per share. Of course, if the index falls, you would only get the $10 original issue price. Always check the participation rate in this type of structure—the higher the better, since a high participation rate leverages your gains if the underlying market or security does well.

Many firms offer mutual funds and other products that carry a principal guarantee structure as well, though you should consider the tax ramifications of any security as part of your research. As they accrue toward their maturity, principal protected products may generate phantom income which you must pay taxes on even though you didn't actually receive income. If this is the case, an IRA or other tax deferred account may be the best place to hold this type of investment. It is wise to discuss any major investment strategy change with both your CPA and your financial advisor before enacting it.

Derivative investments, like options, carry their own risks. Some have unusual tax consequences, potential loss of principal due to the market or the credit of the backer, or have features which could create unexpected volatility. Make sure that you understand any derivative as well as you understand other simpler investments before you use it in your portfolio.

Putting It All Together

12

As I said earlier, information does not necessarily equal understanding. Knowledge of trading strategies, derivatives, and other alternatives in the market can cause more harm than good if they are not backed up with real discipline and an understanding of the basics. So, before enacting anything you have learned here or elsewhere, always consider the basics of investing. The strategies in this book are useless unless they are based on a sound, basic portfolio.

I outlined some guidelines in chapters one through three, and recommend that you read further in that area if you lack experience in the market. The financial language which includes price to earnings ratios, growth rates, debt ratios, dividend yields, asset allocation, and the myriad of other terms related to the market is important to have at least a passing familiarity with. Invest the time to learn about money before you invest your money.

There are several key points in this book that I believe are worth summarizing, in hopes that what you have read will make a real difference in your investing success. Some may seem obvious, but I find that even the most intelligent people I know make the same very human decisions when investing. Here are some points to remember.

Build a high quality portfolio. No amount of strategy, trading, or information can replace the basics of investing in high-quality, well-managed, future-oriented companies. Forget what you have just read until you have built your financial future on the basics. Get qualified professional help if you need to, but make sure the foundation of your portfolio is built on quality, not just on investments that look good in a bull market.

Plan for your future, and let your investments follow. Plan for what you will need to meet your goals, whether they are to retire i n comfort, send four children to college, or buy a new yacht. If through your planning you determine that you need to double your money every year, you need to invest more principal now or adjust your goals. Be realistic, and include the effects of taxes, inflation, and market fluctuations in your planning. I also recommend that most investors obtain the services of a professional. Find someone who is aware of investment alternatives, changes in tax laws, estate planning issues, and many other issues which may help you reach your goals sooner or with less risk.

Begin investing as early as possible. A 30 year old investor should have a very different portfolio that someone who is just about to retire. While much of this book is about controlling risk, don't let fear limit your long term returns. If you are young and have many years of earnings ahead of you, a more aggressive stance is completely appropriate. Conversely, if you are not able to replenish capital that could be lost in the market, you should choose investments with a very low likelihood of loss. Before investing anything, identify who you are as an investor and determine what kind of portfolio is right for you.

Proper asset allocation and diversification reduce risk. This book has hopefully provided some basic ideas as to the different types of assets classes, but you should put some serious thought into what is right for your portfolio. Remember to at least consider all types of assets in your thinking, such as international securities, hard assets/commodities, and real estate.

Asset allocation will determine a large part of your portfolio's return over the long term. A widely quoted study done by Ibbotson Associates revealed the following:

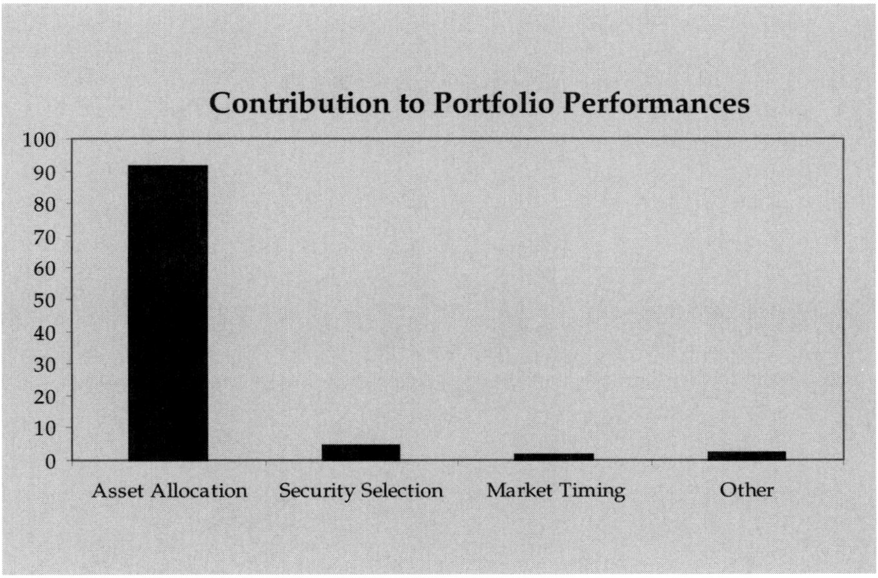

Though it is surprising to most people, asset allocation accounted for 91.5% of the performance (good or bad) in the portfolios studied. Maybe even more, since security selection (4.6%) is arguably a function of asset allocation. Allocation includes placing your assets in different asset classes (bonds, stocks, et cetera), styles (value vs. growth, for instance), and sectors (steel, semiconductors, publishing, et cetera). If the semiconductor sector is experiencing a tremendous rally, you will be experiencing gains with almost any stock in the sector. You will probably do best with the strongest companies in the sector, of course.

The other two factors are essentially negligible in their real effect. Over time, market timing (1.8%) has little effect, because I believe it is impossible to sell at the top and buy at the bottom with any sort of consistency. The "Other" (2.1%) category, which includes trading costs and management fees, can of course grow to a larger percentage when portfolios are turned over too frequently. The basic lesson is that a majority of your time should be spent allocating your assets, not worrying about the market or the smaller costs associated with enacting your portfolio management decisions.

Avoid losses. Remember how insurance works: identify risk, quantify it, then act to reduce its effect on your assets. *Identify, Quantify and Reduce.* Stocks, bonds, and most other investments fluctuate in price. This is a normal part of investing. If you cannot afford to take a loss but can rationally identify risk in an investment, either sell the investment or take other steps to mitigate the loss should it occur. Cut losing investments and let winning investments reach their full potential whenever possible. This is called a sell discipline. Understanding when to sell or hedge is just as important as knowing when and what to buy.

Time in the market is far more important than timing the market. Our natural tendency is to buy at the top and sell at the bottom. Truly successful investors are committed to remain in the market through its ups and downs. Though they may make adjustments in their asset allocation from time to time according to market conditions, they are never out of the market.

It is possible to make money in flat or declining markets. Staying in the market does not necessarily mean gritting your teeth and waiting for better days. It does mean remaining invested and taking steps to make sure your portfolio is properly positioned, and hedged if necessary, for your situation. There are usually at least some investments which are rising when the majority are falling. The opposite is also true—it is very possible to lose money in rising markets. Remember that an index is simply an average of many different investments. If the Dow Jones Industrial Average goes up, it does not mean that every one of the stocks in it rose. As I write this, the Dow Jones Industrial Average is up 20% and the NASDAQ Composite is up 22% year to date. However, 43% of all NASDAQ stocks and 27% of the stocks on the New York Stock Exchange are *down* from where they began the year. In 1994, the NASDAQ Composite fell 3% for the year, yet over 40% of the stocks within it showed a gain for the year! Try to include investments and strategies in your portfolio that will rise or maintain their value when the averages may be falling.

Portfolios managed for instant gratification frequently fail in the long term. Only your own progress towards your goals should matter, so ignore the noise in the market. Adjust your portfolio occasionally, using your investment plan and some basic investment criteria that you believe work for you. If an investment no longer meets the criteria which caused you to buy it, then get rid of it. This may happen frequently, as change is rapid in today's economy and the market. However, make sure you are trading on real fundamentals, not short term fluctuations.

Have the resources you need for success. Today's investor has more information available than ever before. The unprecedented bull market of the past few years has combined with the advent of the internet to make many things available that never have been before. Never has so much been available in the way of raw data. It pays to learn to use these resources because you can never be too informed. However, though I am admittedly biased in saying so, I believe that most investors benefit in using the services of a professional investment advisor as well. There are exceptions to this, such as when the investor is willing to commit to learning all of the things necessary to actually be their own advisor. Since much of what experienced financial consultants know comes through actual gains and losses, the education can be expensive when you are running your own portfolio.

My own bias is towards investment advisors who work on a flat fee basis (no trading commissions or other charges). The charges should generally be between .50 and 2.5% of a portfolio, depending on services required and portfolio size. Fee based management aligns the interests of the broker and the client, so both make more or less money according to the portfolio's performance over time. I also recommend utilizing a financial consultant with one of the larger investment banks. Despite the many changes on Wall Street in the past decade, it is my opinion that these large players are still the primary source of research, new offerings, product inventory, and consistent trading execution for their clients. Hire someone who you trust to offer advice, information, and insight as a part of your financial team, not just a broker to execute trades. Keep in mind that my background and my future are at such a firm, so I am naturally biased. That is for these very reasons. My clients are best served with the capabilities of a true investment bank, not just a place where I can execute trades. Your portfolio is as good as the person who is helping you manage it, so take as much care in selecting your advisor as you would in choosing a doctor. Both professionals will (or should) know everything about your health, whether physical or financial. Like your doctor, your financial advisor should be someone who you trust to make informed decisions which are in your best interest.

During years of restless sleep filled with nightmares of what the market would hand me on the following day, I began to envy my children as they slept. They were oblivious to the financial world that obsessed my thoughts, and were dreaming peacefully while I paced the halls of our home in fits of insomnia. Then, I began to learn that worry need not be a part of investing when you have the proper perspective and information.

Armed with some basics and the strategies in this book, I hope you will be able to invest in the market with a higher degree of comfort than the average investor. The keys to success are discipline and perspective. Ignore the noise that is ever present in the market, keep your eye on the long term, and manage your portfolio in an objective manner. Concentrate on informed opinion and facts. Carefully build your own plan to reach your goals. Your ability to grow and use your assets in the future is all that really matters in the final analysis.

Option Cycle

A

Option symbols use a root symbol to represent the stock or index underlying the option, plus a position to show the month and type of option, and a position to show the strike price:

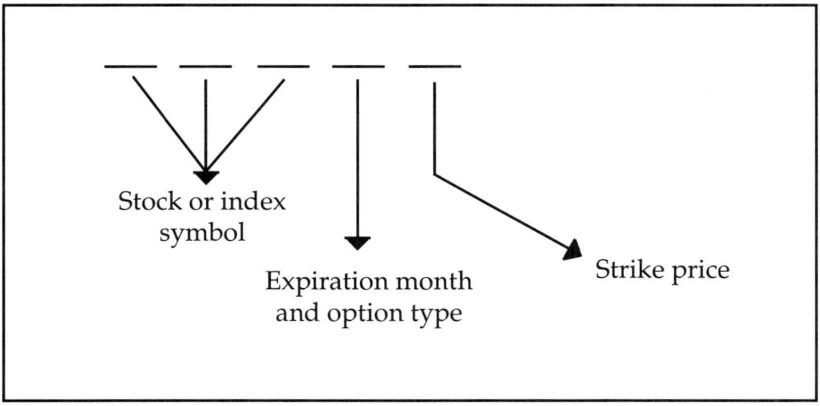

An option's expiration month and type (call or put) are referenced according to the following table:

Expiration Month/Option Type

Month	Jan	Feb	Mar	Apr	May	Jun	Jul	Aug	Sep	Oct	Nov	Dec
Calls:	A	B	C	D	E	F	G	H	I	J	K	L
Puts:	M	N	O	P	Q	R	S	T	U	V	W	X

So, using the letter A would tell you that the option expires in January and is a call, while using the letter M would refer to a put which expires in January.

The last position in an option symbol tells what its strike price is. Note that a single letter referes to multiple strike prices. This is simply because a stock trading at $150 will not have $50 options, since they are so far away from its current price. Generally, use the strike price which is closest to the current price of the stock and you will be correct.

Strike Price

A	B	C	D	E	F	G	H	I	J	K	L	M
5	10	15	20	25	30	35	40	45	50	55	60	65
105	110	115	120	125	130	135	140	145	150	155	160	165

N	O	P	Q	R	S	T	U	V	W	X	Y	Z
70	75	80	85	90	95	100	7.5	12.5	17.5	22.5	27.5	32.5
170	175	180	185	190	195	200						

Options and LEAPS Symbols

B

The following pages contain a sample listing of option and LEAPS symbols. Note that the option root symbol is the same as the stock ticker symbol unless shown otherwise:

Stock	Stock symbol	Option symbol	LEAPS Symbols 1999	2000
Abbott Laboratories	ABT		VBT	LBT
Acuson	ACN		VAU	LAU
Adobe Systems	ADBE	AEQ	BAE	LAE
Advanced Micro Devices	AMD		VVV	LVV
Airtouch Communication	ATI		VRH	LRH
Allied Signal	ALD		VAD	LAL
Allstate	ALL		VLS	LZL
AlteM	ALTR	LTQ	VZT	LZT
Alza	AZA		VZA	LZA
Amerada Hess	AHC		VHS	LHS
Atmel	ATML	AQT	VLH	n/a
AT&T	T		VT	LT
Avon Products	AVP		VVP	LVP
Baker Hughes	BHI		VBH	LBH
Bankamerica	BAC		VBA	LBA
Bank of Boston	BKB		VKB	LBK
Bankers Trust	BT		VET	LET
Barnett Banks	BBI		VRB	LRB
Barrick Gold	ABX		VBX	LBX
Bay Networks	BAY		VLB	LBN
Bell Atlantic	BEL		VBU	LEU
Bell South	BLS		VBL	LBL
Best Buy	BBY		VBY	LBS
Cabletron	CS		VCJ	LCJ
Campbell	CPB		VLL	LLL
Caterpillar	CAT		VKT	LKT
Centocor	CNTO	COQ	VCT	LCO
Chase Manhattan Bank	CMB		VCX	LCK
Chevron	CHV		VCH	LCH
Chiron	CHIR	CIQ	VHR	LHR
Chrysler	C		VCY	LCR
Chubb	CB		VCU	LCU
Cirrus Logic	CRUS	CUQ	VUR	LRL
Dayton Hudson	DH		VDH	LDH
Dell Computer	DELL	DLQ	VDQ	LDE
Delta Air	DAL		VDA	LDA
Digital Equipment	DEC		VDE	LDC
Disney	DIS		VDS	LWD
Dow Chemical	DOW		VDO	LDO
DSC Communications	DIGI	DIQ	VD	LID
Dun and Bradstreet	DNB		VDB	LDB
Dupont	DD		VDD	LDD
Federal Express	FDX		VFX	LFX
Federal National Mortgage	FNM		VFN	LFN
Federated Dept. Stores	FD		VFD	LFD
First Chicago NBD	FCN		VNC	LCD

Stock	Stock symbol	Option symbol	LEAPS Symbols 1999	2000
Ford Motors	F		VFO	LFO
Fore Systems	FORE		VFY	LFY
Fruit of the Loom	FTL	FQO	VTL	LTL
Gap	GPS		VGS	LGS
General Electric	GE		VGE	LGR
General Instruments	GIC		VIY	LIY
General Mills	GIS		VGI	LGI
General Motors	GM		VGN	LGM
Georgia Pacific	GP		VGP	LGP
Gillette	G		VZG	LZG
Glaxo PLC	GLX		VGX	LGX
Goodyear Tire & Rubber	GT		VYR	LYE
Gropo Televisa SA	TV		VVT	LVT
Halliburton	HAL		VHW	n/a
Health south	HRC		VHC	LHH
Heinz	HNZ		VHN	LHN
Hewlett Packard	HWP		VHP	LWP
HFS	HFS		VFS	LFH
Hilton Hotels	HLT		VHL	E~HL
Home Depot	HD		VHD	LHD
Homestake Mining	HM		VHM	LHM
Household International	HI		VOH	LIH
Ikon Offce Solutions	IKN		VKN	LLT
Informix	IFMX	IFQ	VIF	LXF
Intel	INTC	INQ	VNL	LNL
International Business M	IBM		VIB	LIB
International Gaming Tec	IGT		VGG	LGG
International Paper	IP		VNP	LNP
ITT	ITT		VLA	LIP
Johnson & Johnson	JNJ		VJN	LJN
K Mart	KM		VK	LKM
Kroger	KR		VKK	LKK
Eli Lilly	LLY		VIL	LZE
Limited	LTD		VLD	LLD
Lipsome Companies	LIPO	LPQ	VPB	LOF
Lowes Companies	LOW		VOY	LOY
Lucent Technologies	LU		VEU	LUN
Merrill Lynch	MER		VME	LME
Micron Technology	MU		VGY	LGY
Microsoft	MSFT	MSQ	VMF	LMF
Minnesota Mining	MMM		VMU	LMU
Mobil Oil	MOB		VML	LML
Mobile Telecom Technol	MTEL	MMQ	VEM	LEM
Monsanto	MTC		VM	LCT
JP Morgan	JPM		VIP	LJP
Morgan Stanley, DW &	MWD		VWD	LWW

Stock	Stock symbol	Option symbol	LEAPS Symbols 1999	2000
Motorola	MOT		VMA	LMA
National Semiconductor	NSM		VSN	LBV
Nationsbank	NB		VNB	LNB
Newbridge Networks	NN		VNW	LNW
Nextel Communications	NXTL	FQC	VFU	LFU
Nike	NKE		VNK	LNK
Nokia	NOKA	NKA	VOK	LOK
Novell	NOVL	NKQ	VNN	LNO
Occidental Petroleum	OXY		VXY	LXY
Offfice Depot	ODP		VDP	LDP
Oracle Systems	ORCL	ORQ	VOR	LRO
Pairgain Technologies	PAIR	PQG	VGF I	LGC
Pepsi	PEP		VP1	LPP
Pfizer	PFE		VPE	LPE
Pharmacia & Upjohn	PNU		VUP	LUP
Phelps Dodge	PD		VZD	LZD
Philip Morris	MO		VPM	LMO
PHP Healthcare	PPH		VPH	LPH
Pitney Bowes	PBI		VBW	LPI
Placer Dome	PDG		VDG	LPD
Polaroid	PRD		VRD	LRD
Quaker Oats	OAT		VQO	LQO
Qualcomm	QCOM	QAQ	VLM	LLU
Reebok International	RBK		VRK	LRK
Republic Industries	RWIN	WQR	VRW	LPU
RJR Nabisco	RN		VRJ	LRJ
Safeway	SWY		VYW	LYW
Salomon	SB		VSM	LSM
Sara Lee	SLE		VZS	LZS
SBC Communications	SBC		VFE	LFE
Schering Plough	SGP		VSG	LSG
Schlumberger Ltd.	SLB		CWY	LYS
Schwab (Charles)	SCH		VYS	LWS
Seagate Technology	SEG		VTT	LTZ
Sears Roebuck	S		VRS	LS
Signet Banking	SBK		VEP	LEP
Telecommunications	TCOMA	TCQ	VTM	LTE
Telebras	TBR		VZB	LZR
Telefonica Argentina	TAR		VTD	LRA
Telefonos de Mexico	TMX		VTE	LMX
Tenneco	TEN		VTE	LNG
Texaco	TX		VXC	LTO
Texas Instruments	TXN		VXT	LTN
ThreeCom	COMS	THQ	VTH	LTH
Tiffany	TIF		VFF	LFF
UAL (United Air.)	UAL		WA	LUA

Stock	Stock symbol	Option symbol	LEAPS Symbols 1999	LEAPS Symbols 2000
Union Carbide	UK		VCB	LCB
Unisys	UIS		WI	LUI
United Healthcare	UNH		WH	LUH
United Technologies	UTX		VXU	LUD
Unocal	UCL		VCL	LCL
US Air Group	U		VUU	LW
USA Waste Services	UW		VUW	LUY
US Surgical	USS		VSS	LUS
Viacom	VIAB	VMB	VVM	LVM
WalMart	WMT		VWT	LWT
Warner Lambert	WLA		VWL	LWL
Waste Management	MSX		VWM	LWM
Wells Fargo	WFC		VWF	LWF
Wendy's International	WEN		VVE	LVE
Westinghouse	WX		VWX	LWX
Woolworth	Z		VFW	LFW
Worldcom	WCOM	LDQ	VQM	LQM

List of Selected Stock Market Indices

C

Following is a partial list of indices on which options or other types of contracts are traded. You may want to find out which stocks are included and how an index is calculated to evaluate the correlation between any given index and your portfolio.

Index Description	Ticker
Automotive (CBOE)	AUX
Banks (S&P)	BIX
Biotech (AMEX)	BTK
Chemical (S&P)	CEX
Chemicals (S&P)	CEX
Computer Software (CBOE)	CWX
Computer Technology (AMEX)	XCI
Consumer Companies (Morgan Stanley)	CMR
Cyclical Companies (Morgan Stanley)	CYC
Dow Jones Industrial Average	DJX
Dow Jones Transportation Average	DTX
Dow Jones Utility Average	DUX
Environmental (CBOE)	EVX
Gaming (CBOE)	GAX
Gold (CBOE)	GOX
Health Care (S&P)	HCX
Insurance (S&P)	IUX

Index Description	**Ticker**
Internet (CBOE)	INX
Israel (CBOE)	ISX
Japan - Nikkei 300 (CBOE)	NIK
Japan (AMEX)	JPN
Latin America 15 (CBOE)	LTX
Mexico (CBOE)	MEX
Mexico/IPC (CBOE)	MXX
Midcap	MID
Multinational Companies (Morgan Stanley)	NFT
Mutual Funds - Growth (Lipper)	LGO
Mutual Funds - Growth and Income (Lipper)	LIO
NASDAQ 100	NDX
NYSE Composite	NYA
Oil (AMEX)	XOI
Oil (CBOE)	OIX
Pharmaceutical (AMEX)	DRG
Real Estate Investment Trusts (REITs)	RIX
Retail (S&P)	RLX
Russell 2000	RUT
S&P/BARRA Growth	SGX
S&P/BARRA Value	SVX
S&P 100	OEX
S&P 500	SPX
S&P 600	SML
Technology - Composite (Goldman Sachs)	GTC
Technology - Hardware (Goldman Sachs)	GHA
Technology - Internet (Goldman Sachs)	GIN
Technology - Networking (Goldman Sachs)	GIP
Technology - Semiconductors (Goldman Sachs)	GSM
Technology - Services (Goldman Sachs)	GSV
Technology - Software (Goldman Sachs)	GSO
Technology (CBOE)	TXX
Transportation (S&P)	TRX
Telecommunications - US (CBOE)	TCX
Telecommunications - N. America (AMEX)	XTC

Principal Protected Securities and Funds

D

As discussed in the text, each principal protected security has its own specific and often complex terms. The "reference index" is what the security is meant to track, though the degree of participation in that index will vary between securities. Also, remember that many principal protected securities have some sort of tax consequences, the most common of which is "phantom income" which is generated (and taxable) despite the fact that the security may not pay any cash dividends or distributions. There are many other such securities. These are listed on the following page. This is not an inclusive list.

Ticker Symbol	Reference/Benchmark Index	Issue Price ($)	Maturity Date	Minimum Redemption	Issuer
BSL	S&P 500 (SPX)	4.00	5/03	4.00	Bear Stearns
DJM	Dow Jones Indus.Ave.(DJII)	10.00	1/03	10.00	Merrill Lynch
EEM	Major International (EUX)	10.00	12/02	10.00	Merrill Lynch
IEM	S&P 500/inflation adj. (SPX,CPI)	10.00	9/07	10.00	Merrill Lynch
JEM	Japanese Nikkei 225 (NXS)	10.00	6/02	10.00	Merrill Lynch
KBB	Custom Portfolio (XCUB)*	3.00	7/98	3.00	Bear Stearns
MEE	European (MEE)	10.00	6/99	9.00	Merrill Lynch
MEM	Major Euro Markers (EMX)	10.00	8/02	10.00	Merrill Lynch
MIE	S&P 500 (SPX)	10.00	7/98	10.00	Merrill Lynch
MIM	S&P 500 (SPX)	10.00	9/02	10.00	Merrill Lynch
MIX	S&P 500 (SPX)	10.00	5/01	10.00	Merrill Lynch
MLC	Global Telecom (MIGT)	10.00	10/98	9.00	Merrill Lynch
MLH	Biotechnology/Healthcare (MXH)	10.00	10/01	10.00	Merrill Lynch
MPQ	S&P 500 (SPX)	69.55	5/01	69.55	Morgan Stanley
MTT	DJIA "Top 10" (XMT)	10.00	8/06	12.40	Merrill Lynch
NXS	Nikkei 225 (NXS)	10.00	8/02	10.00	Salomon Smith Barney
RUM	Russell 2000 (RUT)	10.00	9/04	10.00	Merrill Lynch
RXS	Russell 2000 (RXS)	10.00	11/04	10.00	Salomon Smith Barney
TKM	Technology (TXX)	10.00	8/01	10.00	Merrill Lynch
XSB	S&P 500 (SPX)	15.00	8/01	15.00	Salomon Smith Barney
YSB	S&P 500 (SPX)	15.00	3/02	15.00	Salomon Smith Barney
ZSB	S&P 500 (SPX)	15.00	2003	15.00	Salomon Smith Barney

* The XCUB portfolio was selected by the issuing company and contains 23 stocks.

Preferred and Convertible Acronyms

E

ACES	Automatic Convertible Equity Securities
ChIPS	Common Stock Higher Income Participation Debt Securities
COPrS	Canadian Originated Preferred Securities
DECS	Debt Exchangeable for Common Stock
ELKS	Equity Linked debt Securities
EPICS	Exchangeable Preferred Income Common Shares
EYES	Enhanced Yield Equity Securities
FRAPS	Fixed/Adjustable Rate Preferred Securities
LEAPS	Long-term Equity Anticipation Securities
LYONS	Liquid Yield Option Notes
MARCS	Mandatory Adjustable Redeemable Convertible Securities
MIDS	Monthly Income Debt Securities
MIPPS	Monthly Income Paying Preferred Securities
PEPS	Participation Equity Preferred Shares
PERCS	Preferred Equity Redemption Cumulative Stock
PERQS	Performance Equity Redemption Quarterly Paid Securities
PRIDES	Preferred Redeemable Increased Dividend Equity Securities
PTOPRS	Perpetual Trust Originated Preferred Securities
QUICS	Quarterly Income Capital Securities
QUIDS	Quarterly Income Debt Securities
QUIPS	Quarterly Income Preferred Securities
SAILS	Stock Appreciation Income Limited Securities
STRYPES	Structured Yield Enhanced Product Exchangeable For Stock
SUNS	Stock Upside Notes Securities
TARGETS	Targeted Enhanced Growth Term Securities
TOPRS	Trust Originated Preferred Securities
TRUPS	Trust and Preferred Stock Power Contract Unit
YEELDS	Yield Exchange Equity Linked Debt Securities

The above securities are each proprietary trademarks of one of the following firms: Goldman Sachs, Lehman Brothers, Merrill Lynch, Smith Barney, or Bear Stears.